ALL IN

A REVOLUTIONARY CALL TO MISSIONAL LEADERSHIP

DREW C. SCHOLL

STREAMLINE
BOOKS

PRAISE FOR ALL IN

It was Shakespeare who said 'some have greatness thrust upon them.' For many, leadership is similarly thrust upon them. As a result, we learn on the fly instead of by design. Drew Scholl teaches us how to become leaders by design—missional leaders. Read, absorb and apply!

— BILL HIGH, 7 GENERATION LEGACY AND LEGACY STONE

Inspiring, challenging, and raw. *All In* calls all of us as Christian Leaders higher. This is an entertaining must read for any leader looking to integrate faith the other six days of the week!

— JOSH WILDMAN, CEO, WILDMAN BUSINESS GROUP

In his book, *All In*, Drew Scholl leads us through his own story of redefining success through faith and focus. He presents a powerful lens for leaders to pursue a full life of purpose.

— MIKE LENDA, CSO, 5BY5 AGENCY

The church today needs a book like *All In*, and I need a book like *All In*. You will be challenged, convicted, and finally come to the realization that maybe we are holding back, hanging on to a life that is ours and not His. You will struggle through the fact that He is worthy and we are better served to live all in for Him no matter the perceived cost!

— KEVIN LARKIN, VP & DIRECTOR OF BUSINESS, GLOBAL SERVE INTERNATIONAL

I've been working with Drew on this for the past decade, unknowingly, and in a way where you live and adventure towards the ideas more so than talk about them. I can tell you this from honest personal experience—Missional leadership is captivating, full of adventure, and will make you feel truly alive. And with Drews personal formula based on his experience of Divine Inspiration + Practical Tools + Personal Discipline—he is more than just a thought leader, he is a trusted guide.

— RILEY FULLER, FOUNDER, HUMANITY AND HOPE
UNITED

This book is dedicated to my amazing wife, Bobbi, of 23 years, and our four children—Gracie, Malachi, Annie, and Levi. Above all, I hope and pray that the storyline of God's work in our lives is a foundation for our kids to build upon and continue our family legacy of faith into future generations.

This book is also dedicated to the legacy of Stephen L. Bryant, a courageous leader, father figure, mentor, and teacher to many. In memory of Steve, February 25, 1949 – December 15, 2023.

CONTENTS

FOREWORD

BY DAVID GREEN

A missional leader is not merely a title, but a calling—a calling to harness God's blessings, and inspire followers, to serve God and lead one's life with focus on God's eternal Kingdom.

Throughout my life, and in the way I have sought to build and grow my business, these principles have been paramount. At Hobby Lobby, we are guided by a steadfast commitment to honor God in all we do, integrate biblical wisdom in our decision-making, and pursue prosperity used to invest in God's Kingdom.

Recently, I wrote a book entitled *Leadership Not by the Book: 12 Unconventional Principles to Drive Incredible Results.* There I sought to capture ideas like Give Away your Profit, Give God the Vote, Give up Ownership, Build for 150 Years, Get in the Weeds. These are the kinds of ideas you don't come across by attending business school. These are the kinds of ideas you come across only as you seek to lead by the Holy Spirit. Being led by the Holy Spirit will not always make sense in the eyes of the world. Yet it is this Holy Spirit-driven leadership that encompasses the missional leader in its truest sense.

It is within the framework of these foundational values that I read Drew Scholl's transformative work—*All In.*

In a world often besieged by uncertainty and disorder, missional leaders can build organizations to provide hope, order, and serve the ultimate certainty of the Good News. Drew Scholl's discerning exploration of this vital subject is timely. Drawing from my own experiences building an organization used for spreading the message of Christ's love, I have found a clear and succinct guide in this book that all missional leaders, and those who aspire to be missional leaders, can rely. It doesn't just provide a roadmap for effective missional leadership but provides solace and inspiration when the inevitable challenges arise.

What distinguishes *All In* is its ability to exhort and equip leaders to embrace the essence of missional leadership, not as a mere course of action, but as a way of life. It is a compelling invitation to our hearts, our hands, and our minds, beckoning us to transcend the ordinary and embark upon a journey in true service to God's Kingdom.

As I reflect on the profound impact of missional leadership within my personal and professional life, I found myself nodding my head in agreement throughout my reading of this book. Drew has done a wonderful job of organizing a path to missional leadership that anyone can follow, and I am enthused to whole-heartedly commend a thorough reading of Drew's book.

—David Green
Founder, Hobby Lobby Stores, Inc.
and author of *Leadership Not By the Book*

INTRODUCTION

At just twenty-five years old, I had achieved enough success to begin designing our dream home. I had been building a division of our family business for about four years, and it seemed like the right time to go for it, so I began designing the biggest, baddest house we could afford—or, at least, *thought* we could afford. I spent months getting the design just right.

With persistence and good salesmanship, I was able to get my wife, Bobbi, fully on board, so we finally took the plunge. We bought a nice piece of property, and I started building our dream home using the design I'd worked on. It was everything we'd ever wanted!

Although we were probably in over our heads, we weren't being neglectful of our other responsibilities, including our spiritual commitments. We tithed faithfully to ministry because we both felt like we should give, at a bare minimum, 10 percent to the work of God's Kingdom. And we didn't enter into this home-building endeavor lightly. I spent countless hours praying about the decision, and it seemed to pass all of the "Christian tests."

In fact, I can look at my prayer journals from that time period and see that I was totally consumed by the project and completely convinced that my wife and I were following the Lord's will. I was pursuing God, yes, but to be perfectly honest, I'm pretty good at justifying just about anything in the name of the Lord. I can see now that I was working hard to convince myself that this house endeavor was God's will. Not just the house, but even the idea of buying other things now, incurring debt and paying later so we could materially have what we wanted. I have learned over the years that we can make the scriptures say whatever we want by simply looking at verses that support our position and ignoring verses that don't quite fit *our* plans.

It's clear to me now that I had one foot in the world and one foot in the Kingdom, and I was trying to serve both. I believe God allowed my wife and I to go down that path, even protected us from financial disaster, because it was an important part of the story he was writing; however, he had a different end in mind than we did. From my perspective, I was building the American Dream, but God knew that in just a few short years he would ask me to give it all up. You see, he had something very different in mind for my wife and I—a journey we would have never imagined.

A Sudden Change of Direction

A few significant events came along and disrupted our direction in life. The first one happened about a year after we moved into our new dream home. Bobbi and I went on our first mission trip, heading down to Honduras with a group called World Compassion Network.

Honduras is the second most populous country in Central America and the second poorest. I had never experienced such crushing poverty before, and it wrecked me. The whole trip was a huge eye-opener, exposing me to a way of life that seemed unthinkable to me. Subsistence living, people with very little just getting by day after day. That blew my mind, but what astounded me even more was the realization that this is how most of the world lives.

In the midst of that poverty, however, I saw the scriptures come to life before my eyes. About halfway through the trip, we got up early one morning to pray together. We had heard stories about people experiencing significant life change on mission trips, but we had not yet experienced a paradigm shift ourselves. As we prayed, we lifted our feelings, emotions, and thoughts to God and asked him to work in our hearts and reveal his word and purpose in all of this. That morning, we fully surrendered ourselves to the Lord's will for our lives, with open hearts and open hands.

As it turned out, one of the Compassion team members I met down there had left a lucrative career as the vice president of a large organization just a year earlier to become a missionary. He had given up almost everything, but he was on fire for the Lord, serving the locals, caring for their needs, and preaching the gospel.

It seemed like such a radical decision to me. Crazy! I was twenty-six years old and gunning hard for growth in our business and my income, and here I was confronted with someone who had given all of that up to serve people in a nonprofit.

I felt extremely convicted by his example and deeply moved by the communities he was serving, and I didn't want to forget any of it. When we returned home, I was flooded with emotion, and I couldn't stop thinking about everything we'd seen and experienced in Honduras. It felt like my life had changed, even though I didn't yet know how it would play out. I had grown my beard out during the trip, and I decided to keep it after I got home as a reminder. To this day, I have not let a razor blade touch my beard.

Honduras was the beginning of a massive change of direction that affected every area of my life. I'll share more of that story later—a story that God continues to write to this day. But the book you're reading right now is a direct result of that new direction and a transformation of my heart that occurred on that mission trip over seventeen years ago. I have a passion to share what's in my heart in the hope that maybe it will inspire others to live differently.

You see, my awakening made me painfully aware of my own self-serving desires. It was like the scales fell off my eyes and I could finally see what was *really* important. Experiencing firsthand the way most of the world lives broke through the pride and selfish ambition that had long guided me, piercing straight to my soul.

It was a new beginning and a new outlook on life, a realization that Jesus transcends cultures and that I had been given so much! How would I leverage what God had given me to make an impact in the world? What if I truly lived all that Jesus taught? That trip planted a seed that has been growing over the last eighteen years. I desire to invite you into this journey of growth, discovery, and life change.

While the book is largely driven by divine inspiration, I hope to include a few practical tools that we can apply to challenge us to greater personal discipline. A good friend of mine read part of this manuscript and sent me a message that said:

Drew = Divine Inspiration + Practical Tools + Personal Discipline.

I was honored by his affirming words and told him I was going to steal this formula and put it in the introduction! Ultimately, my dream is to inspire those in leadership to begin leading courageously and boldly, with radical abandon to Jesus and a total commitment to their role as commissioned Missional Leaders who have been given the ministry of reconciliation. But I want everyone, not just leaders, to live on mission, as men and women sent by God with an attitude like the prophet Isaiah that says, "Here I am, Lord. Send me."

What if the Lord has a radically different plan for our lives than the mundane, worldly, self-serving lifestyle we're tempted to live? Are you willing to let him shake up your thinking? Would you let him change the whole paradigm of your life? What if he wants you to drop everything and head overseas to serve the poor? Or what if he's calling you to go into the world with that same missionary mindset but he has placed you where you are right now to serve him and bring the hope of the gospel?

That's the idea behind Missional Leadership. It's a revolutionary call to live and lead as Jesus would wherever he sends you, whether that's to the ends of earth or right here in your business and family. In the following chapters, we're going to discuss what that might look like, and I encourage you to allow yourself to be challenged, to get a little uncomfortable, because that's the way toward growth and purpose.

Of course, mere words on a page aren't enough to truly make a deep impact in your life, so I pray that the Lord will stir something within you as you take this journey. I hope the Spirit of the Lord will empower you with boldness and courage to more intentionally live a purposeful life that is focused on bringing the hope of the gospel to a lost and dark world.

I'm not trying to position myself as an expert who has figured all of this out. In fact, this book contains questions that I've personally wrestled with for the last twenty years as I've led businesses and teams and spent three years living overseas on the mission field—in many ways, I still wrestle with them as I strive to fully live out what Jesus taught.

The Complexity of Following Christ

As a business leader, I've experienced the complexity of being completely sold-out to Jesus while trying to run a business, but I wonder if it becomes more complex because we make it so. Instead of following what he says, we rationalize and try to soften the impact of his teaching because we want to hold on to some things and maintain control. We want to have it both ways—to follow Jesus *and* to live for the world at the same time.

Running a business is no easy task. It requires wisdom, discernment, courage, a risk-taking attitude, and when the teachings of Jesus seem to compromise those things (from our perspective), it puts us in a real predicament. How can we build profitable businesses that provide for ourselves and our employees if we're radically sold-out to the gospel? Is it even possible?

There's a lot at stake: our family's well-being, our employees and their families, and our customers. It's basic economics, and one bad decision can make a big mess of things. Herein lies the tension!

I still grapple with it, as do many others. But, friends, that's okay. Let's allow ourselves to be challenged, to feel the tension and grapple with it. We try so hard to blunt the sharp edges of Jesus' teaching. We draw lines in the sand and say, "I'll follow him, but only up to this point." Have we forgotten these words of Jesus?

> "Not everyone who says to me, 'Lord, Lord,' will enter the Kingdom of heaven, but only the one who does the will of my Father who is in heaven. Many will say to me on that day, 'Lord, Lord, did we not prophesy in your name and in your name drive out demons and in your name perform many miracles?' Then I will tell them plainly, 'I never knew you. Away from me, you evildoers!'" (Matthew 7:21-23 NIV)[1]

I don't know about you, but I fear those words. I refuse to take them lightly, and I don't want to spend my life thinking I'm doing good only to discover at the end that my heart was never really surrendered to the Lord. I don't want to pay him lip service but keep myself at the center of the story.

And remember these words of the Apostle John:

"We know that we have come to know him if we keep his commands. Whoever says, 'I know him,' but does not do what he commands is a liar, and the truth is not in that person. But if anyone obeys his word, love for God is truly made complete in them" (1 John 2:3-6 NIV).[2]

If we truly belong to Jesus, then it should be evident in the way we live, the things we value, the choices we make. People should see Christ in us in the way we lead our businesses, in the way we serve our families, and in the way we treat other people. Otherwise, our faith becomes a lie, and we need to consider the possibility that we're not really following Him.

Dare to be Challenged

In the upcoming chapters, I'll share with you many stories, some from my own life and some from others, and I pray you will let them challenge, invigorate, and open your eyes to the possibilities. Don't shy away from the discomfort because maybe, just maybe, God is calling you to live your life to the fullest in radical obedience to Jesus Christ wherever you are, wherever he sends you, and with whatever you are doing.

At the end of each chapter, I've provided a few questions for you to prayerfully consider. Let the Lord work deeply in your heart and mind as you contemplate your answers. Let him test, and even threaten, your current paradigm, because he may have something far greater in mind for you than the life you've built for yourself.

Following the Lord fully is not always safe, not always logical, and often runs contrary to the wisdom of the world, but it also changes lives, redeems the lost, brings hope and healing to the broken, and brings light into the darkness.

Say it with me: "Here I am, Lord. Send me."

We call this "Missional Leadership." The word "missional" comes from the Latin word "missio," which means "to send." That's what we are. As followers of Christ, we are sent out into the world with the ministry of reconciliation. Jesus says, "Therefore go and make disciples of all nations, baptizing them in the name of the Father and of the Son and of the Holy Spirit, and teaching them to obey everything I have commanded you."[3] That's our mission, wherever we happen to find ourselves.

If you claim to be a follower of Christ, then you, too, have been called according to his divine purpose, and he is sending you into the world. Embrace this idea and let it permeate every area of your life, whether you're with your family, at work, sitting in traffic, strolling the aisles in the grocery store, or attending a sporting event. It's going to demand some changes to the way you live.

We often marvel at the sacrifices that missionaries make when they are sent onto the foreign mission field, but I think we're all called to make the same sacrifices. Whether you're a missionary, the CEO of an enterprise, or a stay-at-home mom, Jesus is asking you to count the cost, love him more than anything else, and follow him.

Carry your cross, leave everything behind, and follow him. Let's go!

PART I

LIVING MISSIONALLY

1

THE CENTER OF YOUR STORY

How far did God's new direction for my life take me? It took me from an established and progressing career in our family business in the US all the way to the beautiful, rugged mountains of Papua New Guinea. Yes, eventually, his calling drew me and my wife to the mission field, and we found ourselves living in a cabin on the side of a mountain overlooking the Goroka Valley.

Imagine mountains 10,000 to 12,000 feet tall towering over a valley at 5,000 feet. This was the land of the Bena Bena Tribe, and our property in their midst gave us a nearly 360-degree view of our surroundings. How did I wind up all the way on the other side of the world? We'll get to that story a little later. For now, I want to paint the picture.

Every morning, before we turned on the generator, I would wake up while it was still dark and quiet, fire up the stove, heat up water, and make French press coffee. Then I would step out on the front porch for some reading, prayer, and quiet time with God. Often, a gentle haze—a mixture of smoke and clouds—filled the valley, and I would watch it slowly disappear as the sun rose above the crest of the mountain behind me and chased it away. Smoke would seep through the grass rooftops of the local bamboo-walled, dirt-floor huts, as the early morning sounds of our tribal neighbors working their gardens or preparing food echoed across the village.

In the forested valley, Casuarina and Albizia trees towered over coffee gardens, and the air was filled with mysterious bird and animal sounds that were unique to the place. It was a wonderful way to start my day—well, some days. Other days, I awoke with a sense of anxiety, worried about my family's safety in this far-flung place. More on that later, too.

Papua New Guinea is an incredibly diverse island nation with over 865 spoken languages, many of which are unwritten. It requires a lot of patience and a relentless commitment to the Lord's work to endure the years it takes to establish an indigenous church there because missionaries have to learn the unwritten local language and culture. After learning the language and culture, missionaries have to develop a written version of the language and teach the people to read it, so they can begin the long, meticulous process of translating the Bible. And that doesn't even take into consideration all the hours of teaching, discipleship, raising up local church leaders, and caring for people's needs.

We went to Papua New Guinea to help run a mobilization program called Interface that was part of the church-planting organization Ethnos360. As part of that work, we hosted six-week programs for college students at our camp situated in the Bena Bena tribe. Students came from around the world, and our goal was to give them a full picture of the amount of time, effort, and perseverance it takes to plant a church among one of the least reached people groups. Ultimately, we wanted the program to challenge them to become part of God's plan for bringing the gospel to every nation, tribe, and tongue.

We had a few families who were full-time staff members, and we had some interns from Germany who came and stayed with us for a year at a time thanks to a program set up with Germany that enabled young adults to take a gap year after high school. We were blessed to mentor two or three young Germans each year we lived there, and we built great relationships with them. Our kids especially loved them.

One year, the German interns kept asking us to take them to the coast because they had never swum in the Pacific Ocean. We seldom went down to the coast due to logistical challenges. PNG has almost no safe roads in the interior, and there was only a single road that led from our area to the coast. It was a difficult drive, to put it mildly. But when my brother Matt came to visit our family on the mission field, I figured it was a great opportunity to make the difficult trek. I could spend time with my brother, the interns would get to snorkel in the Pacific, and everyone would have a great time.

Due to limited space and safety concerns, my wife was more than happy to stay behind on our peaceful mountain while I ventured off into the unknown. The three German interns and my brother helped me load our bags, and then we picked up one additional passenger from our village, a local named Michael. He showed up ready for the four-day trip with only the clothes on his back, a bilum (similar to a purse) with a few bucks, and a giant machete. I thought I'd packed light with my full backpack and my knife, but Michael was a real man's man. I felt so much less macho in his presence.

Michael had never swum in the ocean, and he'd never snorkeled, so we wanted to give him a chance to do that. However, to be honest, we also brought him as a security measure. It's rarely a good idea to travel in PNG without a local who can read the crowd and situations, and that single highway is often targeted by thieves. Since it's the only road to the coast, it's often traversed by container trucks bringing supplies up to Goroka—tempting targets for rascally people.

Before we departed our village, Michael decorated our vehicle with banana leaves and kunai grass so we looked local—you know, *less* noticeable (even though we looked like a giant plant on wheels).

We spent seven adventurous hours driving on the highway, 190 miles of winding insanity, past precarious drops and over a million bumps. Fortunately, we eventually arrived, intact and unharmed, in the coastal town of Madang.

We decided to head to a place called Pig Island, which sits two miles off the coast of Madang. We made arrangements with a water taxi to take us there and pick up again at a certain time. All of the islands in the area are dense with jungle that runs right up onto the sandy shores, and it was a bit disconcerting to realize that the water taxi could easily strand us there. We'd have no way to get back to Madang. Swimming across two miles of open ocean in the South Pacific wasn't really an option.

We hadn't paid the guy yet, so we just had to hope that he would come back for his money. But ultimately, our safety was in his hands. As we approached Pig Island, we saw massive coconut trees and palm trees towering over white sand. The water close to the island was a vibrant blue, with coral visible just beneath the surface.

The water taxi landed on the shore and dropped us off. We said a friendly, "Lukim yu bihain," to the captain (that's "see you later" in Tok Pisin, a local creole language), and the water taxi headed back to Madang. Aside from one other PNG native we spotted in the distance, we were the only human beings on the small island that day, and as the boat sped off into the distance, I felt a moment of trepidation. It felt a bit like we'd just become castaways.

The doubt only lasted a few seconds, as I was quickly captivated by our beautiful surroundings and the amazing adventure that awaited us. The snorkeling turned out to be a truly epic experience, with the best underwater views I've ever seen. The coral off Pig Island was bursting with color, and we saw some of the craziest-looking fish, creatures of all shapes and colors.

We floated on the surface for hours, our faces in the water, occasionally diving down fifteen to twenty feet to get a closer look at the coral as we drifted further from the shore. Michael struggled with the concept of snorkeling, and we shared many laughs as he choked and sputtered while trying to make it work. Eventually, he just got rid of the snorkel and held his breath. Even as a local, he was blown away by the view. He'd had no idea such beautiful things lay just off the coast of his unique and mysterious country.

Now, my skin usually handles the sun quite well. I don't burn easily. That said, I was still concerned about exposing my back to the sun all day, especially with the sunlight being amplified by the water, so my brother and I wore t-shirts, and we cautioned the German guys to wear t-shirts as well. One of them heeded our advice, the other two did not, claiming that sunscreen was enough. They were adults, eighteen and nineteen, so I didn't push the issue too hard.

From time to time, we swam back to shore and took a break. We'd lean against a coconut tree in the shade and recount the beauty of God's creation which we'd seen with our own eyes. I also pointed out to the two German guys, "Hey, you two are starting to look a little red. Maybe you should put your shirts on now." And every time, they would reply, "Ah, we're fine. We're tough guys. We can handle it."

As the day drew to a close, our trusty water taxi appeared on the horizon. He hadn't abandoned us after all. We were picked up and brought back safely to Madang, and we spent the evening sharing stories of our adventure, laughing a lot, and enjoying fellowship.

I'm a musician and singer/songwriter, so I captured all of my reflections about the day in a song called "I See in the Sea." It was a simple ukulele song that shared the beauty of our adventure on Pig Island. You can check it out on Spotify. If you find a song with that title and like it, then you've probably found the right one. If you don't like it, then it must be someone else's song with the same title (ha!).

But, man oh man, the sunburns! Those two German guys were burnt to a crisp! The sun had destroyed their backs, shoulders, arms, and legs, and red skin turned to blisters and a whole lot of pain. I offered some sympathetic words, but at the same time, I'd tried to warn them. They could only lie down on their bellies, and they couldn't really sit comfortably in chairs. The bumpy ride back up the mountains on that harrowing highway to Goroka proved especially painful.

The Genius and Precision of God

Isn't it amazing how much of an impact the sun has on us? It's 93 million miles away from the earth. To put that in perspective, if you took a road trip to the sun, had never-ending fuel, and averaged sixty miles an hour, it would take you 176 years to get there. That's such an impossible distance to wrap my head around.

However, that distance is important to our survival. In fact, it's just perfect for sustaining life on the earth. The surface of the sun is a toasty 10,340 degrees Fahrenheit. If the earth's orbit shifted just a little bit closer to the sun, glaciers would melt, sea levels would rise, most of the landmasses on the planet would be flooded, and there would be sunburns all around! But if the earth drifted just a little farther from the sun, oceans would freeze, ecosystems would die, and we'd enter an ice age from which we might never recover.

As it turns out, we are just the right distance—not too close, not too far

—to enjoy the life-sustaining warmth and light from the sun, so plants and animals can thrive all across the globe (as long as some of them wear t-shirts when snorkeling all day). The genius and precision of God is astonishing, really. Consider the fact that, as you read this book right now, you are currently spinning about 1,000 miles per hour on a ball that is hurtling through space. The ground at your feet is just a thin crust covering a massive inner core that's nearly as hot as the sun, and the surface of the planet around you is about 71 percent water.

Somehow, despite spinning constantly, this force called gravity is keeping you, all of that water, and everything else from flying off into outer space. If that's not crazy enough, consider the fact that this spinning ball is also orbiting a gigantic ball of fire called the sun at about 67,000 miles per hour (that's 18.5 miles a *second*)—and it's just at the perfect distance from that fireball to make life possible.

Personally, when I look at the beauty and precision of creation, I am both amazed and convinced that there is an intelligent, purposeful design to all of this. On those mornings when I would sit on my porch in Papua New Guinea and gaze at the mountains, listening to those majestic and unique birds, I was reminded of God's power and his breathtaking creation. When I ponder science and all of the things that are beyond what we can see, it only increases my sense of wonder.

"The Heavens declare the glory of God; the skies proclaim the work of his hands. Day after day they pour forth speech; night after night they display knowledge. There is no speech or language where their voice is not heard. Their voice goes out into all the earth, their words to the ends of the earth. In the heavens he has pitched a tent for the sun, which is like a bridegroom coming forth from his pavilion, like a champion rejoicing to run his course. It rises at one end of the heavens and makes its circuit to the other; nothing is hidden from its heat" (Psalm 19:1-4 NIV).[1]

And yet, despite all of this, I sometimes think (and act) like the whole world revolves around *me*. As if I were the sun. But don't we all do this sometimes? We get so consumed with how we feel, how we look, how we're doing: do we have enough money, do we have enough friends, are we making an impact, are we working out hard enough, are we going bald?

If I could install some kind of tracking mechanism in my brain, I bet I'd be embarrassed to discover just how much I think about myself. C.S. Lewis in his book, *Mere Christianity*, and Rick Warren in *Purpose Driven Life*, both talk about this idea of how much we think of ourselves and present the challenge of thinking of ourselves less, while not thinking less of ourselves. Man, that's a hard thing to do, isn't it?

Imagine if you were hired as an extra in a movie scene. Extras are generally nonverbal background performers. They're in a scene to make it look more realistic, but they don't speak. They don't draw attention to themselves. They make up the patrons in the background of crowded restaurants, or on sidewalks, or at the mall.

My favorite movie of all time is the Jack Black comedy *Nacho Libre*. Let's suppose you were hired to be an extra in the crowd of cheering fans in the climactic scene where Nacho gets a chance to fight the great Ramses. If you've seen the movie, you'll remember there's a moment where he uses his eagle powers to jump from the top rope, fly through the air, and tackle Ramses, who is attempting to run away like a coward.

As an extra, let's say you're one of several hundred people in the crowd as he flies through the air, but you're off in the distance near the top of the arena. Ultimately, you appear in the movie for about half a second as Jack Black flies by, and that's it. If you look really hard, you can spot yourself.

But let's suppose you are so pumped about appearing in a movie with Jack Black that you invite all of your friends and family to attend the debut. In the days leading up to the showing, you brag to family and friends about your amazing role in this movie. You get as many tickets as you can and hand them out to people.

And as you sit there in the darkened theater, surrounded by dozens of friends and family members, you watch the movie unfold with mounting anticipation. You keep turning to them and whispering, "It's coming, guys. My scene is almost here! Get ready!"

Then it happens. Jack Black flies off the top rope, the music swells, and you appear way in the background for half a second. "Wow, look at me," you cry. "There I am! Do you see me? There I am!"

You pass by so quickly that many of your friends don't even see you, and those who do really aren't impressed at all. That's it? That's your big appearance in the movie? In the end, your mom may be proud of you, and your eleven-year-old son might think it's cool, but most people don't really care and couldn't even tell you were there.

Here's the thing: you were not at the center of the movie. *Nacho Libre* wasn't about you. Yes, you had the distinct privilege of playing a very small role in the movie, but your contribution was tiny. Nevertheless, you made a huge deal about it. You massively overinflated your importance to the movie and wound up embarrassing yourself.

This may seem like a ridiculous scenario, but if we are honest with ourselves, that's what so many of us do in life. We think and talk and act like the whole world revolves around us when, in fact, we play a tiny, tiny role in the grand scheme of things. Our individual lives are like a blip, a fraction of time in a great movie that is ultimately about God. Even so, it's amazing that you get to be an extra in that much bigger story, and you should be excited that you appeared even for a fraction of a second. What an honor!

The movie of life is about what God is doing from eternity. Any chance we get to serve the majestic Creator, who made both the sun we revolve around and the son who saves us, should always be placed at the center of all things. We revolve around him, not the other way around.

We are given this short life, this blip in time, that is a part of an ancient narrative spanning thousands of years and still playing out at this moment with a clearly scripted picture of what is yet to come. Each breath, each second, each action is part of this storyline.

From cover to cover, the Bible captures the story. If you haven't read it, you should. From Genesis through Revelation, it's clearly God's story about his progressive revelation of who he is and his unfolding redemptive plan to deliver wayward people through the promise of a savior. The Old Testament points ahead to a deliverer sent by God, and in the New Testament, that deliverer is revealed as God's one and only son, Jesus Christ, who was sent to the earth so that whoever believes in him shall not perish but have eternal life.

God the Father has made Jesus, his son, the center of the story. We revolve around him, and what an honor it is to play any part, however small, in the unfolding of that great redemptive story.

Whom Shall I Send?

So what part are we called to play in God's great redemptive story? Well, before we can answer that question, we have to acknowledge that there's a problem. You see, we are broken vessels and bring nothing to the table of eternal significance apart from a relationship with Christ. John 15:5 says apart from him we can do nothing, so if we're going to play a role, any role at all, we have to begin with a willingness to yield entirely to the purposes of God. He must do the work of repairing these broken vessels so they can serve him.

Ephesians 2:8-10 says that "it is by grace we have been saved, through faith, and this is not of ourselves, it is the gift of God, not by works so that no one can boast."[2] In other words, God does it. He does the work in us and through us. We just have to be willing, available, and obedient.

Think about the people God used in the scriptures to spread the gospel and grow his Kingdom. Very few of them came from prominent positions of power. Most started off as ordinary people doing ordinary jobs, like fishermen and tax collectors. God seems to like choosing the lowly and humble in order to display his power. That's certainly true of the Apostles.

Knowing this should give you the confidence that if you will fully trust God to work in you and through you by his own power, then he can and will accomplish great things. What if it were possible to have some sense of his manifest presence in every area of your life?

Remember, Jesus didn't die for some and ignore others. His death was a payment made for all the sins of humanity so that those who place their faith in Him can be wholly restored and used by Him anywhere they happen to be. I believe God has sprinkled us all over the world like salt because he wants to raise us up in communities and cultures and far-flung places. Jesus calls us "the salt of the earth" because, like salt, we are to bring the flavor of the gospel wherever we are. Your life is to add the flavor of the gospel to your community, to your culture, to the place where you are, to your family.

The great work of Jesus isn't just for other people. God didn't overlook you when making his plans. He has a role for you, uniquely you, in the unfolding story that revolves around him. You are a commissioned ambassador of Christ, and he wants the power of the gospel to be fully displayed in you. Yes, you. Consider the following scriptures:

"[For God] made his light shine in our hearts to give us the light of the knowledge of the glory of God in the face of Christ. But we have this treasure in jars of clay to show that this all-surpassing power is from God and not from us" (2 Corinthians 4:6b-7 NIV)[3].

"Therefore, if anyone is in Christ, the new creation has come: The old has gone, the new is here! All this is from God, who reconciled us to himself through Christ and gave us the ministry of reconciliation: that God was reconciling the world to himself in Christ, not counting people's sins against them. And he has committed to us the message of reconciliation. We are therefore Christ's ambassadors, as though God were making his appeal through us. We implore you on Christ's behalf: Be reconciled to God. God made him who had no sin to be sin for us, so that in him we might become the righteousness of God. As God's co-workers we urge you not to receive God's grace in vain" (2 Corinthians 5:17-6:1 NIV)[4].

Let that sink in. We are ambassadors. All of us, no matter how mundane you think your life is. Executive, janitor, missionary, stay-at-home mom, it doesn't matter. We're all Christ's ambassadors. However small we are in the big scheme of what God is doing, we all have a role to play. Another passage I would encourage you to read is 1 Corinthians 3:5-9. In it, Paul makes clear that every individual has a role to play, but the Lord assigns each person their task. Some, he says, prepare the soil. Others plant the seed. Some water. But, importantly, God is the one who ultimately makes it grow.

As Paul writes, "So neither the one who plants nor the one who waters is anything, but only God, who makes things grow. The one who plants and the one who waters have one purpose, and they will each be rewarded according to their own labor. For we are co-workers in God's service; you are God's field, God's building" (1 Corinthians 3:7-9 NIV)[5].

No matter who you are, God wants to work through you in some way, alongside your co-laborers in Christ, to make the gospel grow in the hearts of men and women around the world. What an honor it is to play any part at all in that great work! There is none greater.

So what would it look like if today you decided to become more intentional about living missionally, and surrendered not just part, but every area of your life so you could be all God designed you to be? What if God has so much more for you as part of his master plan to redeem the world? There is no greater joy than when we lay aside our own agenda and fully commit to be co-laborers in Christ, embracing God's purpose of glorifying himself among the nations. What may seem uncomfortable or costly at the time will soon fade as you realize true fulfillment, experience his goodness, and discover that it's all worth it.

I've spent two decades working in the marketplace and three years as an overseas missionary. I have lived both a ministry vocation and a non-ministry vocation. You might think it's more spiritual, more "on mission," to sell everything you have, give up the comforts of home, and move to a jungle on the other side of the world.

To be honest, I thought so, too, when I first made the transition from business to the overseas mission field. When God called me back into the business world three years later, to the same business I'd left behind when I went into ministry, initially it felt like I was making a less spiritual decision. But I was wrong. God wanted to work through me just as much in the business as he did on that mountaintop in Goroka. He was just as present, just as powerful, and had just as much purpose for my life.

In all places, at all times, God asks, "Whom shall I send? And who will go for us?" The prophet Isaiah's answer to that question was, "Here I am, Lord. Send me." He had an eagerness to serve God. What about you?

The location, vocation, and occupation don't matter. Wherever you are, and wherever God sends you, He wants you to be on mission and faithfully pursuing everything that He has for you. Where you are and where you work doesn't make you more or less spiritual. If you're all in and sold-out completely to Jesus and His work in you, then there will be an outflow of His Spirit wherever you are. Jesus said, "I am the vine, you are the branches. If you remain in me and I in you, you will bear much fruit; apart from me you can do nothing" (John 15:5 NIV)[6].

So what would your life look like—at home, at work, wherever—if you were, right this minute, fully and completely committed to Jesus, fully and completely available to His work of spreading the gospel, and if you put Him at the very center of everything? Dare to consider what this might look like.

Questions to Prayerfully Consider

- As you reflect on this chapter, who would you say is at the center of your story? What if Jesus was the center of your story? What would change?

- Is He at the very center of your home life? Is He at the very center of your work life? How would your life look differently if this were so?

- Are you fully available to God so that He might work through you wherever you happen to be? What is standing in the way? What is holding you back?

- In what ways could you add the flavor of the gospel to your community, work culture, and family?

- Have you considered the fact that as a Christian you are a commissioned ambassador of Christ, given the ministry of reconciliation? How might embracing this truth impact your life and your mission?

2

BURNING YOUR SHIPS

Hernán Cortés was a Spanish conquistador and explorer whose travels in the early 16th century brought about the downfall of the Aztec empire and put much of Mexico under the rule of the king of Castile. Now, before I get into his story, I want to note that I'm using this historical event as a metaphor. Please don't take this as any kind of endorsement of the mission or some of the methods used by Cortés against the indigenous people of Mexico.

I mention him now because he did something audacious on his first expedition that shows such a boldness in his leadership that I think we can all learn from it. Cortés was relentless in his pursuit of the mission, determined to see victory and win the prize of Mexico for his royal benefactor. He set sail for the New World in 1504 with a fleet of eleven ships packed with 500 soldiers and 100 sailors, all of whom were explorers and treasure seekers at heart.

As a leader, Cortés was charismatic and inspirational, but he had little practical military experience. He made up for this with a determination to conquer, and he drew around himself a group of followers who were inspired by his tenacity. After brief forays in Hispaniola and Cuba, Cortés finally landed on the American mainland in March 1519 with no idea of what he and his men were about to face.

Though his men were courageous and committed, Cortés wanted to make sure that no one would entertain any thoughts of fleeing or returning home if and when they met with resistance from hostile Mesoamerican forces. Therefore, he did something that might seem utterly insane: he ordered his men to burn all of the ships.

It was a bold move by Cortés. I can imagine him rallying his men and saying, We are going to be victorious and see this mission all the way through. We won't turn back because we *can't* turn back. All that remains to us now is the mission, and we either conquer or we die.

It was a radical abandonment of rationality, logic, and back-up plans and a relentless commitment to complete the mission that he felt he'd been called to fulfill. I'm not endorsing the mission of the conquistadors, their lust for gold, or their severity with indigenous people, but I do feel inspired by a commitment that would willingly cut off any chance of easy escape.

I imagine they would think, "Now, we have to see this through because there's no way back."

What if we applied that level of commitment to a far better mission?

A Tale of Two Churches

In Luke 9:57-62, Jesus speaks to a few people who say they want to follow him. In each instance, these well-intentioned individuals express a desire to follow Jesus but request to fulfill some other obligations first:[1]

"Lord, first let me go and bury my father."

"I will follow you, Lord; but first let me go back and say goodbye to my family."

In verse 62, Jesus replies to them rather harshly, "No one who puts a hand to the plow and looks back is fit for service in the kingdom of God."

Consider that response for a moment. It's not hard to imagine Jesus saying, "Remember when Cortés burned his ships? I want you to burn your ships. Count the cost and fully commit, because anyone who climbs back on board the ship to safety isn't fit for the Kingdom of God."

Burning your ships, putting your hand to the plow and not looking back, not saying goodbye to your family first—all of these speak to hard sacrifices and heavy costs. Clearly, what Jesus teaches is not for the faint of heart, the half-committed, or those who want the best of both worlds.

That was the struggle for the church in Laodicea. They wanted the best of both worlds. Jesus has a word for this: *lukewarm*. Revelation 3:14-22 is a huge wakeup call from Jesus to the church—and to us. Get your Bible right now and read it. It's powerful, convicting, and challenging.

In the passage, Jesus says, "I know your deeds, that you are neither cold nor hot. I wish you were either one or the other! So, because you are lukewarm—neither hot nor cold—I am about to spit you out of my mouth" (Rev. 3:14-22 NIV)[2]. Brutal.

Do we just gloss over this passage? It doesn't feel good, but it's not supposed to. It's clearly intended as a shocking wake-up call to anyone who reads it. Think about what Jesus is saying here. Let it sink in: "Fully commit or don't commit, but make up your mind, or I'm done with you." If that doesn't make you tremble a little bit, then you're not really taking it in.

In Isaiah 29:13, God says something similar: "These people come near to me with their mouth and honor me with their lips, but their hearts are far from me."[3] This is what it looks like to be lukewarm—paying lip service to God but not actually yielding our hearts to him. Being lukewarm is doing some Christian things in your life, like going to church or praying occasionally, without your heart being fully sold-out to Jesus. God is very clear how he feels about this.

The Bible is full of stories of God's people drifting away from him, being wayward, seeking worldly things, falling away—and being desperately in need of a deliverer to bring them back to God. That's the beauty of God's love and grace. He doesn't just spew us out of his mouth. He also reaches out and draws us back.

Look at what he says to the church in Laodicea. In Revelation 3:17, he calls them "wretched, pitiful, poor, blind, and naked." That's harsh, but he doesn't leave it there. He then says, "Those whom I love I rebuke and discipline. So be earnest and repent. Here I am! I stand at the door and knock. If anyone hears my voice and opens the door, I will come in and eat with him, and he with me. To him who overcomes, I will give the right to sit with me on my throne."

So, am I saying there's hope for all of those lukewarm, half-committed Christians that God wants to spit out of his mouth? Yes, absolutely. Be earnest and repent. Open the door fully to Jesus. Follow Him with a full commitment and don't look back. Let the ships burn. Jesus has something much better for you ahead.

If you've never read the book *Crazy Love* by Francis Chan, I strongly encourage you to buy the book as soon as possible and read it, particularly the chapter called "Profile of the Lukewarm." That book contributed to the massive paradigm shift in my life that began in Honduras, and that chapter deals very effectively with the same topic we're talking about here. Just be ready to be challenged hard.

Now, having examined the lukewarm church in Laodicea, let's take a look at a far better example. In Revelation 3:7-13, Jesus speaks to the church at Philadelphia, a church that shows us a clear picture of what we should strive to be. Rather than threatening to spit them out of his mouth, Jesus tells them, "I know you have little strength, yet you have kept my word and have not denied my name."

He goes on to say that he will provide for them, show the world his love for them, and keep them from the "hour of trial" that is to come upon the whole world. He's clearly proud of them and loves their faithfulness in following him.

2 Chronicles 16:9 says, "The eyes of the Lord range throughout the earth to strengthen those whose hearts are fully committed to him."[4] We see this very thing happening in Jesus' response to the church in Philadelphia.

Ironically, they have little strength of their own—they are lowly and humble—but the Lord sees their devotion and strengthens them. I imagine they had little in the way of worldly possession, not much to offer anybody other than the gospel. They probably lived simple and modest lives but gave what little they had to meet needs with generous hearts. They faced trials of many kinds, but they stood firm in their faith through them all. As a result, they found favor with the Lord.

Laodicea, on the other hand, had plenty of worldly treasures. They were wealthy and comfortable, lacked nothing, and felt proud about it. As we would say today, they were living the good life. They were going to church and saying all the right Christian things, looking like followers of Jesus outwardly, but inside, their commitment to him was weak, flimsy, and half-hearted.

I'll be completely honest with you. When I read about Laodicea, it cuts deep. I don't want to be a proud, self-satisfied, comfortable, half-committed, lukewarm follower of Jesus, and I know I have been. At the same time, I'm inspired by the church at Philadelphia, and I feel honored and grateful that I have the opportunity to humbly serve a God who invites us to follow him with wild abandon.

Escape the Mundane

Maybe the idea of "wild abandon" seems silly to you because your life feels mundane. You have a job, you might have a spouse and kids, bills to pay—it's all very ordinary. What's the point of being all in for Jesus? It's not like he's going to do anything amazing through you.

I understand that feeling. There have been times in my life where I felt like I was just going through the motions. Just living a dull, ordinary life. Looking back, I realize I was simply distracted by the things of this world and failing to see God at work all around me right there in the ordinariness. I was caught up in work, trying to get projects done, and pursuing worldly interests that ultimately left me unfulfilled.

God wanted to use me to do amazing things right where I was, but I was too distracted to make myself available to him. I'd put my hand to the plow, but I was looking back. Maybe you're in the same place. Hey, I get it. Making yourself wholly available to God is scary. He might require some hard decisions, sacrifices, and trials, and all of those things are uncomfortable. When we feel uncomfortable, we tend to retreat to the mundane.

But, listen, if you will focus solely on what God is doing and where he's leading, totally committed to Jesus, he's going to help you overcome this timidity. I'm telling you from experience, if you will seek him first above all else, he's going to give you such fulfillment and contentment that you'll feel bolder and more courageous than you've ever felt. The life he's calling you to doesn't depend on you. God is going to give you everything you need to live a godly, meaningful life. He just wants your commitment and availability.

The secret of going from mundane to meaningful lies in removing ourselves from the center of the story, going from no longer being a consumer Christian or seeking fulfillment in the world to following God in everything. He has wired each of us for a specific purpose, and when we pursue that purpose, we enjoy a deep sense of fulfillment that nothing else can bring. We also get to contribute some small part to God's ultimate purpose.

We will never find that same fulfillment apart from the call of Christ in our lives, and if we never fully commit to his purpose, we will always feel like we are profoundly lacking something—and some people, sadly, will discover that this awful feeling can last for eternity.

So when did I finally burn my own ships? I think I set fire to them while my wife and I were in Honduras. We came back from that trip knowing we could never go back to a mundane life. Practically speaking, however, we spent the next few years unpacking what it really means to be all in for Jesus and how our lives should reflect that commitment. I'll share more of that journey in the last chapter.

The parable of the rich young ruler from Mark 10:17-27 challenged me deeply. It seemed like my wife and I were doing all the right things, genuinely pursuing God and his will for our lives, but he gradually revealed that we hadn't yet yielded everything to him. We faced many tests to our commitment, but our commitment to the Lord will always be tested in this world. And any little part of us that we hold back, any ship left unburned, can become a place of conflict between God's purpose and our worldly pursuits, a place of retreat from his fulfilling will.

We are still working through that today, and likely will for the rest of our lives. There have been and will be several more "burn our ships" opportunities. Why? Because even though we have burned our ships and committed to God an action, way of life, or decision, we often slowly start building new ships over time, filling them with new stuff—things we think we need for the journey. It's being tempted by new idols, putting anything but God at the center. Slowly and subtly, and I would even say subconsciously, we make a way to retreat from God's will.

We are all prone to wander, prone to be pulled back into our sinful state of self-dependence (aka lukewarmth). We are continually lured by the Laodecians to come back to their church.

Yes, burning our ships is a lifelong process. It's why Jesus says to carry our cross daily. Each day we must die to ourselves to follow him and burn anything in the way. Or as the author of Hebrews says, throw off everything that hinders and the sin that so easily entangles us. It's always uncomfortable and requires some element of sacrifice. But I can assure you one thing: it is the most fulfilling thing you can do. So much joy, blessing, fun, and adventure await you on the other side of the ship-burning party!

So let them all burn. Leave no ship behind, no avenue of retreat from moving forward with Jesus to whatever great purpose he calls you.

Questions to Prayerfully Consider

- What if you burned your ships? What ships (things of self dependence, self-serving pursuits, anything that is taking the place of God in your life) would need to burn? What things are you still holding onto that you know he wants you to surrender or leave behind?

- Do you relate more to the church of Laodicea or the church of Philadelphia? In what ways might you be living a lukewarm faith?

- Have you fully committed your life to Jesus and his will for your life? What is holding you back from being all in? What are you afraid will happen if you're radically sold out to him?

- How do you think your life would look different if you were fully devoted to Christ in everything? How might it impact how you lead?

3

THE FIRST PRIORITY

What was looking to be a decent day ended up being a bad dream for the Ironman athletes. It started raining hard early in the morning and didn't let up throughout the entire race. Winds were blowing at a brisk fifteen to twenty miles per hour, and the temperatures were in the low-fifties.

The Madison, Wisconsin Ironman is known to have unpredictable weather on race day, but no one had ever seen one quite like this. The day was emotionally, mentally, and physically grueling. Even so, I felt a fierce determination to keep going, to persevere and reach the finish line. Nearly a third of the athletes dropped out or did not finish, but in my mind, quitting simply wasn't an option, even though I was tempted to give up many times. So many others were giving up, I thought, so why shouldn't I?

I'd never been so cold and wet; I'd never shivered so hard for so long. None of us were prepared to endure such relentless weather. Even my insanely tough seventy-year-old father-in-law, who had entered the race with me, was struggling. During the long biking portion of the race, my hands went stiff and numb from the rain, wind, and cold. I was afraid that if I got a flat, I wouldn't be able to change the tire.

Seven hours into the biking portion, my father-in-law and I reached the transition point, where we left our bikes and prepared for the marathon, at roughly the same time. Thankfully, the transition took place inside the convention center, but when we walked inside, it looked like a morgue. Athletes were sprawled all over the place, shivering, wrapped in aluminum blankets, and struggling to get warm.

Many of them didn't bother going back out, and as I stripped and wrung the water out of my sopping wet shirt, I was tempted to do the same. I wrapped myself in an aluminum blanket and wrestled with the decision. In the end, my determination to press on won out. I decided to forget what was behind me and focus on the finish line ahead, to finish the race that had been marked out for me, weather and all. So after a long twenty minutes in transition, I dressed again and trudged back out into the cold, bitter rain to begin the long, miserable marathon.

By the time evening began to settle in, I found myself lumbering among many other zombies in the final miles of the race. Other than the howling wind, the rustling tree branches, and rain splashing on the pavement, the streets were quieter than usual for an Ironman event. Since so many participants had dropped out, it began to feel lonely and eerie.

As I got closer to downtown Madison, I heard a voice in the distance coming from a PA system: "You are an Ironman!" The announcer was shouting it out every time an athlete crossed the finish line. These long-anticipated words began to pierce my soul as the echo rang out over my surroundings, and they gave me a burst of renewed energy.

When I reached the last few hundred yards, I heard the few remaining courageous spectators cheering me on, including my wife, ten-year-old son, and mother-in-law who endured the elements all day, which kept me going all the way to the end. Finally, I crossed the finish line and heard the thrilling words, "Drew Scholl, you are an Ironman!" It was an awesome moment. I'd completed a 2.4-mile swim, a 112-mile bicycle ride, and a 26.2-mile marathon and finished my first full Ironman triathlon.

The Ironman triathlon is a grueling experience that people pay to participate in. It's a nice chunk of change just to enter the race, but then you have to pay for the gear and nutrition you need to train and race. There's also the cost of travel and lodging. It's not cheap, so hopefully it's your dream vacation! And what do I have to show for all of that? A beat-up pair of Hoka shoes, some empty Cliff Bar boxes, a medal, and, most importantly, a profound sense of accomplishment.

Now, during the race, when the misery was at its worst, I swore I would never do another triathlon, but afterward, as the days went by, the memories of pain and misery began to fade. Gradually, I felt a yearning to try again, so when I had a chance to sign up for Ironman Lake Placid the following summer, I jumped at the chance. My father-in-law, who had suffered that miserable race in Madison with me, also signed up, as did my eighteen-year-old son, and a friend of ours. Because misery loves company, right?

The Ironman Lake Placid race happened this past July (at the time of this writing), and three generations, along with our friend, endured a long bike race through the Adirondack mountains—one of the most brutal Ironman bike courses in the US. The weather was beautiful this time—no rain, little wind, nice temperatures—but it turned into another difficult slog, this time for a completely different reason.

I made, shall we say, a "nutrition mistake" before the race and during the bike portion, and it wreaked havoc on my digestive system. The worst of it hit toward the end of the bike race and stayed with me throughout the entire marathon. Again, I was sorely tempted to quit, but I hung in there, mostly because I didn't want my wife to pick on me if I gave up because of a "wittle tummyache." I had to dig deep to keep going toward the finish line (not to mention the Porta Potties and bushes).

I made it to the finish line, but during the last half of the race, I kept telling myself, "I'm never doing this again! No more triathlons! No way! I'm done!" And here I am just a few months later, signed up for Ironman Canada.

Why? Why do I keep doing this to myself? The Ironman Triathlon is generally considered the single most difficult day-long sport in the world, but there's a good reason why I've completed two of them, as well as seven of the half distance 70.3 Ironman events. There's a reason why I continue to sign up for more.

You see, nearly every facet of the race—the preparation, training, equipment, nutrition, the cost, the race itself, the celebration, the suffering and disappointment, the perseverance—it all reminds of what it's like to meaningfully and intentionally follow Jesus, to run the race that he has marked out for me. It's a metaphor for my life! A physical representation of relentlessly pursuing something much bigger than me.

Keep Going!

In his letter to the Romans, the Apostle Paul tells us that suffering produces perseverance, perseverance produces character, and character produces hope. The idea is that when we grow weary, when we feel like quitting, we keep going because we trust that God is doing good and beautiful and holy work in us, in our lives, and through us. In other words, it's all going to be worth it!

That should motivate us to keep our eyes fixed on the finish line so we keep pushing and *finish well*. The discipline it takes to get there is never pleasant while we're going through it, but we are determined to reach the end of the race because we want to feel the celebration of victory. I persevered and conquered the Ironman, finished the race, and received a medal to memorialize the victory.

But here's the critical question.

If I will do this for a temporary prize, how much more should I train, prepare, and persevere to complete something that will last forever?

In 2 Corinthians, Paul says, "That is why we never give up. Though our bodies are dying, our spirits are being renewed every day. For our present troubles are small and won't last very long. Yet they produce for us a glory that vastly outweighs them and will last forever! So we don't look at the troubles we can see now; rather, we fix our gaze on things that cannot be seen. For the things we see now will soon be gone, but the things we cannot see will last forever" (2 Corinthians 4:16-18 NLT)[1].

We train our bodies in an effort to fight the inevitable decay that comes with aging, but the spiritual disciplines don't decay!

My determination to complete these excruciating endurance tests didn't start with the Ironman. I've had seasons of intense physical activity throughout my life. When I was younger, that usually manifested as a Saturday morning run. Even then, I was pushing myself in the same way, enduring discomfort for the sake of completing the goal. And even then, I was thinking about the spiritual metaphor of it all.

That same level of physical discipline may not be for everyone. In fact, it might not even be safe, especially if you have certain kinds of disabilities, an old injury, or some other condition. However, I do recommend pursuing some kind of physical activity that is suitable for you and making it part of your routine (as long as you're able to). Embrace it as a gift while you can. I thank God every day for my ability to be physically active because I know perfectly well it could change at any time due to age or injury.

I encourage you to care for your body, not only because your body is a temple of the Holy Spirit, but because physical activity can sharpen your mind, increase your mental toughness, and most importantly, remind you to apply even greater discipline to win the eternal crown and the heavenly prize God is calling you to. If you're able to, start by competing in a local 5K, even if you have to walk the entire race. The idea is to set a goal that will challenge you mentally and physically so you can push yourself and learn endurance.

Having said that, I believe (and so does Paul) we should apply the same level of discipline and energy to pursuing Jesus, who endured the agony and discipline of the cross in order to win the ultimate victory and cross the greatest finishing line—for you, for me, for a broken and lost world, in order to produce a harvest of righteousness and peace. When we cross the spiritual finish line, we get to live in eternal harmony with our King.

So, how about you? Are you training to finish the race that will win you the eternal prize? Are you running with perseverance in the race that God has marked out for you? Consider this chapter my way of cheering you on, just like the crowd (and the guy on the PA) cheered for me as I reached the finish line.

The Invitation

The Bible talks repeatedly about the Holy Spirit and the power of God working in us, but what do these verses really mean? How do we harness that power and His presence in our lives, especially if we're going to persevere all the way to the finish line?

Unfortunately, we live in a Western culture that moves quickly, demands fast service, and is full of hustle and bustle. If you're a parent, then there's a good chance your kids are involved in youth sports, but even youth sports have become highly competitive. It's not just playing games at school anymore. Now, sports clubs have kids traveling to games, pushing hard to win tournaments, playing on Sunday, and training intensely to win—and at younger and younger ages. Beyond that, there are plenty of other school activities and extracurricular activities demanding their time.

It has become harder than ever for families to gather consistently around the dinner table in the evening, which should be a sacred place for conversation and connection. At work, we're struggling to get "caught up," battling a relentless onslaught of projects, emails, messages, and problems, while still trying to somehow juggle family issues, family vehicle problems, problems with your house, weather, and whatever else.

Our lives are full of distraction and busyness, but how much of it matters? How much of our time is wasted on activities of no eternal value? When it comes to our spiritual lives, if we do anything at all, we settle for a five-minute devotion so that we can check the box and move on. And that's if we make any time at all.

But that's a bit like choosing McDonald's as your only source of nutrition when you could choose a gourmet meal. Not just any gourmet meal, but a meal with the King of the Universe, who has set out a spread of goodness and delight that comprise the most nutritious meal possible. A meal that will sustain you and provide health and longevity.

In Luke, Jesus tells a parable that illustrates this.

> "'Blessed is everyone who will eat bread in the Kingdom of God!' But he said to him, 'A man once gave a great banquet and invited many. And at the time for the banquet, he sent his servant to say to those who had been invited, 'Come, for everything is now ready.' But they all alike began to make excuses. The first said to him, 'I have bought a field, and I must go out and see it. Please have me excused.' And another said, 'I have bought five yoke of oxen, and I go to examine them. Please have me excused.' Still another said, 'I just got married, so I can't come" (Luke 14:15-24 ESV)[2].

All of these people give good reasons why they can't come to the banquet, but we have our excuses, don't we? Busy at work, busy in personal life, too many chores, so much we need to do.

And what is Jesus' response to these excuses?

"The master told the servant to go out and invite others from the alleys and the streets and bring back the poor, the crippled, the blind, and the lame."

Remember, Jesus is telling this parable to a religious pharisee and the type of people he was saying to invite were considered lowly sinners and outcasts by the religious community. Yet this is exactly who he invited to the banquet. Or, as he says elsewhere, "Blessed are the poor in spirit, for theirs is the Kingdom of heaven" (Matthew 5:3 NIV)[3].

In other words, it's the humble, the people who freely admit their need for Jesus and his mercy, who hear the invitation and set aside everything to respond. People like the church in Philadelphia.

And who does Jesus say will *not* get to join him at his eternal banquet? People who decline the invitation to come in and dine and enjoy his presence because *they are too busy*. Maybe those for whom God is simply an add-on, not a necessity, like the lukewarm people of Laodicea. Ouch!

In other words, there's a lot at stake here, a lot to gain and a lot to lose, so this isn't something we should treat as an "add on" or "bonus." In Revelation, there is a scene where Jesus is standing at the door knocking, waiting for us to respond to his voice and open the door so he can come in and dine with us. How do we pause all of life's noise, distractions, and happenings so we can get to the door and let him in?

And if Jesus *did* walk into your house today, how much time would you give him? Five minutes? What if he walked into your house *every* day with the express intention of sitting down with you to chat?

"Jesus, I can only chat with you for five minutes. I'm sorry, but I'm just so busy."

His invitation and presence in our life has so much more to offer than any of those other things that occupy our time. Think about that image of a banquet. What does it convey? A lot of good things. Just think about a nearly endless array of delicious food and drinks spread out before us, and we get to enjoy it all.

That's the image Jesus uses to depict what is waiting for us if we'll respond to his invitation and let him in! Best of all, we get Jesus himself, present and powerful in our lives! So, it's time for a gut check about your priorities. Read the following statement and allow it to challenge you:

We make time for whatever is important to us.

How we spend our money and our time is a direct reflection of our priorities. If you want to build a relationship with someone, what is the single most important thing you have to contribute? Time. How do you get to know someone? Spend more time with them!

What would your relationship with your spouse be like—or your best friend or another loved one—if you only spent five minutes with them a couple of times a week? What if you thought about them throughout the day but you never actually sat down and intentionally had a conversation with them? Your relationship would start to wane, and eventually you might not have a relationship with them at all.

But that's a fair comparison with how many of us treat our relationship with God. He has invited us to share eternal life with him, and we rarely give him more than the occasional five-minute quiet time—if that! Shouldn't we spend plenty of real, intentional time *every day* in conversation with him, both speaking (through prayer) and listening (through the scriptures and the Holy Spirit within)?

How do we *truly* come to know God? By experiencing his presence and entering into a deep and profound relationship with him. That's how we love him with all of our heart, mind, soul, and strength. Think about your best relationships. What do those relationships entail? They include vulnerability, venting, sharing your thoughts, sometimes crying, maybe getting angry. Sometimes, they hold you accountable, give advice, point you in a different direction, or just comfort you in your pain.

Why should our relationship with God be any different?

We see an excellent example of a relationship in the story of God and "the man after God's own heart," King David. In many of the Psalms, you can see David crying out to God, sharing his emotions, and journaling about his frustrations and doubts. He also writes songs of praise, meditates on scriptures, seeks wisdom, and prayers. Look at the following examples:

- Psalm 77 – David crying out to God.
- Psalms 95-105 – David praising God.
- Psalm 119:33 – David asking for wisdom.
- Psalm 56 – David expressing his trust in God.
- Psalm 64 – David's complaint against God.
- Psalm 43 – David questioning God.

In Matthew 6:33, Jesus tells us to seek first his Kingdom and his righteousness and all of the other things we need will be given to us. He tells us in that same passage not to worry about our basic, practical needs but to seek him first and trust him to work out everything for his purpose and glory. A tough challenge, I know, but it's the challenge that has been presented to us.

So what are we doing to draw closer to him? To seek him first and make time for building our relationship with him? Well, I would like to give you a few ideas that might encourage you to meet this challenge.

From Discipline to Desire

As with training for any athletic competition, you need discipline, consistency, and training time in order to prepare yourself to compete and reach the finish line. Merely thinking about the Ironman triathlon is not enough. Spending five minutes a day doing ab work won't be enough either. There's no fast-food nutrition plan to get you ready, and no shortcuts. If you expect to make it all the way to the end of the race and finish well, you must be disciplined and put in the work.

The athletic metaphor transcends time and culture. Almost 3,000 years before Christ, the Ancient Egyptians were involved in sports both for recreation and training for war. The Apostle Paul used athletics as a metaphor and a recurring theme in his writings throughout the New Testament.

The Olympic and Isthmian Games were intense competitions in those days, not for the faint of heart or the casual runner. Competitors were required to swear that they had trained diligently for at least ten months. Winning—or even just competing—demanded passion, purpose, and a singular drive to win. Paul would have been familiar with these games, and perhaps they were on his mind when he used the metaphor of running a race.

For example, this is what he writes in 1 Corinthians 9:24-27 (NLT):

"Don't you realize that in a race everyone runs, but only one
person gets the prize? So run to win! All athletes are disciplined in
their training. They do it to win a prize that will fade away, but we

do it for an eternal prize. So I run with purpose in every step. I am not just shadowboxing. I discipline my body like an athlete, training it to do what it should. Otherwise, I fear that after preaching to others I myself might be disqualified."[4]

We could spend a lot of time digging into this scripture and others like it, but this is just one book after all. I encourage you to study this passage and others like it (check out the footnote) for additional context and insight into what Paul is teaching. Mostly, I want to focus on what these passages tell us about being disciplined in pursuing Christ.

If you're an athlete, do you apply equal or greater focus on your relationship with Jesus?

If you're a gamer, do you apply equal or greater focus?

If you're a musician, writer, disc golfer, TV binger, social media nut, whatever your hobby is that you make intentional time for, do you spend, could you spend, should you spend as much time dedicated to the most important relationship you will ever have in your life?

We often say we don't have enough time due to work, family, school, and various difficult things, but what about the things we choose to do? What about our hobbies? Somehow, most of us make time for those. We still manage to watch TV and movies, play games, work on some craft, play golf, or whatever it happens to be. There's nothing wrong with a hobby, but if we still manage to carve out time for these pursuits in the midst of our busyness, why do we find it impossible to do the same for our most important relationship?

It reminds me of our tribal friends in the village in Papua New Guinea. Often, they would tell me they didn't have enough money for this or that, but then I would see them pull a wad of kina out of their pocket later the same day.

Eventually, I pointed this out to a buddy. "Hey, you said you didn't have any money to pay for a truck ride into town, but later you pulled out a wad of kina. What gives?"

He explained to me that the kina in his pocket was for something else he was planning to buy. In his mind, since he had already allocated it, that money was as good as spent and not available for a less important purchase that he still might want. From his perspective, he had no money, even though he technically had cash in his pocket. We do something similar with time. We've already allocated time for various activities in our mind, so we act like we have no time when, practically speaking, we do.

The enemy uses distraction to keep us from God. It's an effective tool particularly against westerners because it's gentle and subtle, and our culture provides plenty of distractions. 2 Corinthians 11:14 tells us that "Satan disguises himself as an angel of light," and he does this to draw us to things that might look good but turn our focus away from the real Light. Before we know it, all of our time, focus, and priorities have been consumed by activities of little eternal value, and we fail to focus on the one relationship that matters most. We fail to spend time with Jesus, learning to abide in the Holy Spirit.

In this kind of environment, with so much meaningful stuff to consume our time and attention, how do we develop the discipline for spiritual growth? I believe the most important part of the answer is that we must root ourselves in a love for Jesus. All of this, the entire premise of going all in for Jesus, is based on our response to his love for us.

He loved us (mankind) first even though we were and are rebellious and we're continually building new ships of self dependence and safety instead of being wholly dependent on him and all that he has for us. While we were still sinners he sent his son to take the place of our sin, our rebellion, and our desire for things other than him. When we truly understand his love, his grace, his mercy, it produces a response of love and adoration for him, which produces a desire to know him, which produces a desire to be obedient to him.

In the absence of a foundation of love, spiritual discipline can easily become self-righteous, pharisaical, or legalistic.

If our desire for growth is rooted in a love for Jesus, then it changes our priorities and, therefore, our behavior. It's not about the level of holiness or self-control we can achieve through our own hard work and effort. Rather, it's a desire for a true transformation of the heart that produces obedience to the object of our love, and ultimately creates the fruit of righteousness.

If that's what we're striving for, then there are a few things we should do.

Steps to Discipline

First, we need to **commit** to making time, carving it out of our current schedules in any way possible, to spend time building our relationship with God and growing in our knowledge of him.

For me, it's most effective to do this in the morning because I can always control what time I wake up. It's also what Jesus did. We see in the Gospel accounts that Jesus would get up early while it was quiet and go to solitary places and pray. Try getting up fifteen minutes earlier and using the extra time to spend with God in prayer, Bible study, and reflection. Then, gradually increase it to thirty minutes, then to 45 minutes, and so on.

Maybe you already have the extra time in the morning, but you spend it on consuming news or social media. I strongly encourage you to trade some of that time and spend it with God instead. Consuming media might be informational and entertaining, but it can also pollute your mind. Andy Stanley wrote a great book about this years ago called *Choosing to Cheat*. In it, he points out that time is a limited commodity, so something is bound to get cheated of your time. What are you choosing to cheat? Shouldn't the most important thing in your life—your relationship with Jesus—get priority?

I've found that my early morning calibration is one of the most impactful parts of my day. Because I start my morning with the Lord, it impacts the decisions I make, the actions I take, and the impact I have on others throughout the day, simply by filling me with light before I head out. When I miss out on my morning quiet time and just go straight into my day, I'm a different person. I live more like the wretched sinner that I am, conforming to the world and its idea of who I should be.

To be clear, I'm not saying the quiet time makes me less of a sinner. Rather, it helps to transform me "by the renewing of my mind" so I am better able to "test and approve what God's will is—his good, pleasing and perfect will" as I go about my day (Romans 12:2 NIV)[5].

Second, once you've committed to making time, you need to learn how to **focus** that time. How you spend your time with God is personal, but it's more fruitful to focus on things that are particularly meaningful to your spiritual growth. That doesn't mean you need to create some rigid, legalistic structure with no room for the Spirit to move or no ability to adjust according to your season of life or what's on your mind.

To help you make the most of your time with the Lord, I'd like to share some Biblical disciplines I've learned and developed over the years. This is not meant to be prescriptive, nor do we have the time for an exhaustive deep dive. However, I hope a high-level overview will inspire you to action, but I've included some scripture references if you want to explore these topics more.

Scripture Meditation

Deuteronomy 17:18-19, Joshua 1:7-8, Psalms 1:1-3, Psalms 78:1-8, Psalms 119, Proverbs 1:1-7, Proverbs 4:20-22, Isaiah 8:20, Isaiah 26:3, Colossians 1:9-14, James 1:22

We become what we feed ourselves.

If you desire to follow Jesus, then you need to know what God has to say to us through the Bible. It's as simple as that. James encourages us to listen to the word and do what it says. The Scriptures are the foundation for knowing God personally and intimately and learning His will for our lives.

His word is called "a lamp for my feet" and a "light for my path." It's the compass set to True North, and the only way we can validate what God is saying to us. It is our ultimate authority, and the only absolute truth. It is the source for discovering who we are as a people and our true identity.

It is the moral compass that guides and directs our steps. It is "living and active, sharper than any double-edged sword, it penetrates even to dividing soul and spirit, joints and marrow; it judges the thoughts and attitudes of the heart" (Hebrew 4:12 ESV)[6]. It is "God-breathed and useful for teaching, rebuking, correcting and training in righteousness," so that we "may be thoroughly equipped for every good work" (2 Tim 3:16 NIV)[7].

Prayer and Journaling

1 Samuel 12:19-23, Daniel 9:1-19, Matthew 6:6-13, Mark 11:22, Luke 5:15-16, Luke 11:9-13, Romans 8:26-27, Philippians 1:1-11, Philippians 4:6-7, Colossians 4:12,

James 5:13-18, 1 John 5:14-15. Also, Psalms and Lamentations are great examples of journaling prayers and thoughts to God.

I started writing out my prayer requests in a list format over twenty years ago. The list slowly evolved into writing more about each request, and then eventually it became a full-blown journal. These days, I write my prayers in a way that's similar to the Psalms, including requests, thanksgiving, expressions of grief, celebration, and struggle, the processing of thoughts, and so on. They resemble letters to God, and I use them as a way of focusing my prayers and choosing my words.

Along the way, I decided to start all of my prayers with a sentence or two of thanksgiving for all of God's provisions the previous day. Then I move into whatever is on my heart and mind, whether that's a lament, frustration, a cry for help for my kids or loved ones, rejoicing over an answered prayer, a request for missionaries we support, a situation at work, or a conversation I know I'll have later in the day.

I write it all out like a letter to God, then I'll often re-read it, pausing at times in quietness to listen and maybe write a response or inspiration the Lord lays on my heart. Sometimes, I reflect on a scripture I read that day and write my thoughts in prayer form, ask questions, or even express frustration and confusion. This prayer journaling is one of the most significant contributors to my mental health, my soul's well-being, and my spiritual communion with God, and I look forward to it every day. Just me, my journal, my Bible, and a fresh cup of French-pressed Generous coffee.

One great thing about journaling my prayers is that I'm able to look back through them and observe recurring themes. In some cases, I've seen themes that spanned five to ten years! I also see consistencies in how God is speaking, leading, and moving, and I can reflect on my times of distress or spiritual malaise to see how God pulled me through tough situations. Things I wrote years ago can minister to me and encourage me in situations I'm going through today.

When it came to writing this book, I poured through my journals looking for insights and revelations from certain seasons of my life, like the stories I've shared from my time in Papua New Guinea. Indeed, many of the ideas I present in this book began in some seed-form in my prayer journal.

If you've never tried setting aside time to write out your prayers, I highly recommend it. Give it a try. It may just transform the way you live and deepen your relationship with God in ways you never imagined.

Silence, Solitude, and Listening

Psalm 46:10, Psalm 62, Isaiah 30:15, Matthew 11:28-30, 14:13, 14:23, 26:39, Mark 1:35, 6:31-32, James 1:19, Luke 4:42, 5:15-16, 6:12-13

One of the most effective and impactful spiritual disciplines is simply spending time being still before the Lord. It sounds easy, but many people find it incredibly hard to do. Jesus practiced this discipline himself. Multiple times in the Gospel accounts, we read that Jesus went away, sought solitude, and spent time with the Father—sometimes praying all night.

There are many different forms of silence, solitude, and listening. At the most basic level, it's just sitting quietly in a meditative state. If you want to practice this discipline, start with three minutes. Set a time on your phone, then sit quietly, focusing on an image of God that keeps your attention. Let your busy mind settle and all thoughts that enter pass by like swift-moving clouds.

In a sense, you are emptying yourself in order to give full space for the presence of God to permeate all of your being. Three minutes is merely a starting point so you can make it part of your daily routine, but eventually, I recommend increasing the time to five minutes, then ten minutes, and so on. You might find time to get away for a few hours on a long walk, or take a day trip where you spend extended time in quietness, solitude, and listening.

One of my favorite illustrations of the power of spending time being still before God comes from an experiment using a jar of water and sediment. Here's how it works:

Take a clear jar and fill it with water. Mix in a little dirt or sand. Swirl it around until the water becomes brown and murky. Then let the jar sit for a while and watch as the sediment slowly settles to the bottom and the water becomes clear again.

When we are hustling, bustling, busy, stressed, and living life, our minds and hearts become as murky as the swirling water in that jar. We can't see clearly, we can't think clearly, and we are limited in our ability to receive the fresh water that Jesus offers us. However, when we come before God and enter his presence, sit sometimes for an uncomfortable amount of time, the swirling sediment of the world gradually sinks away and our minds and hearts become clear.

This, my friends, is an excellent illustration of Romans 12:2.

"Do not be conformed to this world, but be transformed by the renewal of your mind, that by testing you may discern what is the will of God, what is good and acceptable and perfect."[8]

Cheering You On

Hopefully, some of the ideas I've shared in this chapter inspire you. Just remember, I am cheering you on in the race God has marked out for you and the discipline and training you endure to finish the race well.

Just as an athlete makes time to train and improve their performance in a sport, so we should make time to train, focus, and be disciplined in our spiritual lives so we may run the race and finish well. Recall these words of Paul:

> "Therefore since we are surrounded by such a great cloud of witnesses, let us throw off everything that hinders and the sin that so easily entangles, and let us run with perseverance the race marked out for us. Let us fix our eyes on Jesus the author and perfector of our faith, who for the joy set before him endured the cross, scorning its shame, and sat down at the right hand of the throne of God. Consider him who endured such opposition from sinful men so that you will not grow weary and lose heart" (Hebrews 12:1-3 NIV)[9].

As we wrap up this chapter, I want to go a little deeper into the idea of hearing from God and receiving inspiration from the Holy Spirit.

It happens in the stillness, in the quiet, when we have communion with God. Rarely do we hear from him in the busyness of the day, when our minds are full of noise and distraction. Even our prayers can get too chattery; we expound on all of our needs and stresses. While this is good, and God wants to hear from us, he also wants us to be still, to know him and allow his presence and voice to be heard. Communication goes both ways, so we need to listen to God as much as we lift up our prayer requests.

One of my favorite illustrations from scripture about hearing God's voice in the stillness comes from a story in 1 Kings chapter 19. To get the full context, I encourage you to read 1 Kings 18:16 to 1 Kings 19:18. To summarize the story, Elijah had just seen God do some amazing things through him, which caused the corrupt King Ahab's wife Jezebel to send death threats to him, so he fled to the hill country to escape her wrath and save his own life.

He then travels on for forty days until he reaches Horeb, the Mountain of God, the same mountain where God had given the Ten Commandments to Moses four centuries earlier. God finally speaks to Elijah and asks, "What are you doing here?" And Elijah, desperate for God's grace, pours out his woes.

God tells Elijah to go and stand on the mountain for the presence of the Lord is about to pass by. And then we read this:

> "Then a great and powerful wind tore the mountains apart and
> shattered the rocks before the Lord but the Lord was not in the
> wind. After the wind there was an earthquake, but the Lord was
> not in the earthquake. After the earthquake came a fire, but the
> Lord was not in the fire. And after the fire came a gentle whisper.
> When Elijah heard it he pulled his cloak over his face and went out
> and stood at the mouth of the cave" (1 Kings 19:11-12 NIV)[10].

Instead of using the phrase "a gentle whisper," the NRSV translation calls it "the sound of sheer silence." I'm blown away by that image of God's presence there with Elijah. God creates this tender moment in the midst of all these grand displays of power and violence, letting Elijah enjoy his peace, and it's in this moment, in the quiet and stillness, that Elijah is able to hear from the Lord and clearly discern what he should do next.

Jezebel is still trying to kill him. What's changed is that Elijah can now more clearly feel God's presence and hear him. God cares for his people, then and now, and he still speaks to us mostly in a still, small voice. Our powerful, majestic Creator desires to have a relationship with us. The same powerful voice that spoke creation into existence also speaks to us personally and intimately, and blesses us with his peace and presence. How could anything possibly compare? Knowing this should change your life!

Consider the following verses:

Philippians 4:6-7 NIV, "Do not be anxious about anything, but in every situation, by prayer and petition, with thanksgiving, present your requests to God. And the peace of God, which transcends all understanding, will guard your hearts and your minds in Christ Jesus."[11]

Psalm 46:10 NIV, "Be Still and know that I am God."[12]

Psalm 27:14 NIV, "Wait for the Lord; be strong and take heart and wait for the Lord."[13]

If we don't prioritize taking the time to come before the Lord in the quietness and stillness, then we may never experience the full, intimate, relationship presence of God in the midst of our noisy, busy lives. It's as critical to our spiritual lives as breathing is to our physical lives.

God is always present. He is everywhere all the time, but until we acknowledge his presence and quiet ourselves before him, we will not experience his presence. Shut out everything else and listen. That's where we feel him. That's where we hear him.

To be clear, God speaks to us in many ways, and he deals with individuals in different ways. He can choose to speak to you in any way he sees fit. However, scripture makes clear that we open ourselves to experience his wonderful presence most powerfully when we learn the discipline of quieting ourselves and coming before him.

Begin taking intentional steps to spend more time pursuing Jesus and building that relationship. Make it the first priority because it will change your life, transform your heart, and equip you to inspire life change in others.

Questions to Prayerfully Consider

- What if your relationship with God was the most important relationship you'll ever have?

- What are you choosing to cheat? Where does building a relationship with God fall in your priorities?

- Do you spend as much time with God as you do social media or news? What are you filling yourself with? (In a later chapter, we'll examine how what you fill yourself with is what comes out to others.)

- Do you believe that we make time for whatever is important to us? What are some simple changes you could make to create more time for God?

- What new disciplines do you need to create in order to best prepare to finish the race that is marked out for you?

4

MISSIONAL FAMILY

L iving purposefully as a follower of Christ should permeate every area of our lives. How we engage in relationships with other people, including how we lead at work, how we parent, and how we treat our spouses, should reflect Christ. We're sometimes willing to see ourselves as ambassadors of Christ when we're on the mission field or doing some charitable work, but we often fail to look through the same lens when it comes to our relationships with friends, family, our children, and other close loved ones.

In this chapter, I want to take a look at the missional family. We'll break it up into three sections: being a **missional single**, having a **missional marriage**, and practicing **missional parenting**.

Missional Single

A few months ago, I had the opportunity to take my family to Kenya to serve with an organization called Kutoa Project, which provides counseling and care for Kenyans who have been affected by trauma. The founder asked me if I would be willing to come and take their Kenyan leadership team through a two-day leadership and team-building workshop. I am thankful we said yes!

My family enjoyed the opportunity and it was impactful to see the work Kutoa Project is doing firsthand. We have supported them financially for a number of years. My wife is on the board and had been there before, but I had not yet been to Kenya to see the work. Like many amazing nonprofits, this organization was started by a young, single woman with a vision that stemmed from a broken heart and humble beginnings. It was amazing to see the work they are doing today because of her courage.

Just out of college, Shaé Brown packed her bags for Kenya to work with a missions agency. She summoned up her courage and made the flight. She soon found herself in uncomfortable circumstances that grew and stretched her as a person. A few years later, when she was twenty-four, she felt called to start her own ministry, which she named Kutoa Project. I asked her about this experience as a single woman, and this is what she said:

"God showed me parts of myself when I was single that laid the foundation for my life and shaped my experiences in a way that, if I would have waited to serve as a missionary until I was married, I would have missed out on some unique experiences God had for me. He showed me how to set boundaries, how to fight injustice (Micah 6:8), how to serve Him in a way where I had all the flexibility and openness to try new things and be part of things, to be bold and courageous (Joshua 1:9), and to lean on Him in times of trouble.

"I think back to my time as a single and all that I was able to do. I worked for one organization where I traveled to rural Kenya and would camp out in the community and disciple the women there and help them share the gospel to those they served. My colleagues with children couldn't easily do this for days at a time but I could and I loved it. I was able to work with girls who have been rescued from a life of human trafficking, and I served them during their healing process. I worked in a slum area of Kenya where I was able to go into people's homes and help them get resources they needed and connect with a church family. I volunteered at children's homes to understand the need for mental health services to those living in group settings. I was able to mentor and start soccer programs in another city of Kenya, serving young girls and discipling young adults to use their gift of coaching and sports to share the gospel and create avenues for these girls to thrive in their community.

"I was able to be the founder of Kutoa Project and travel back and forth to Kenya to figure out the best way to use my giftings to serve children and young adults who have experienced trauma, to know they are seen, heard, and loved by God, and to provide resources for them to find healing."

Shaé leveraged the power of her singleness to make an impact with what God had given her in that season of her life.

Some people marry young, others marry later in life, some lose their spouses, and some never marry. No matter the marital circumstances, if Christ is central to you, and if your relationship with him is the most important relationship in your life, then he can and will do incredible things through you. He may even take you to the ends of the earth to play a role in bringing the gospel to a remote language group!

We can have lives that are wholly pleasing to God and bring glory to his name whether we're married, widowed, have children, or never have children.

Missional Marriage

My wife's parents, Brent and Karen, are amazing people. They've been married for forty-nine years, and they both have hearts that desire to serve the Lord and make him known. They have demonstrated this in so many ways over the years. Their house has been open to hundreds, if not thousands, and they have touched countless lives, establishing a legacy of godly purpose and ministry.

About ten years ago, they purchased a vacation rental as an investment property on the island of Kauai. Though it is rented out most of the year, they reserve the property for themselves from January to March. If you've never been, Kauai is quite possibly the closest thing to heaven on earth. It is stunningly beautiful and is what I imagine the Garden of Eden might have looked like.

During the months they spend in Kauai, they host people 90 percent of the time. They'll often have one group leave, and then another group come in the same day or very next day.

For the last ten years, they've hosted marriage retreats at their home. Well over a hundred couples have gone through these retreats, where they learn to deepen their relationships and, more importantly, discuss the principles of "marriage as mission." So many couples have been impacted by this amazing ministry experience.

Brent and Karen are missional in almost everything they do. They support missionaries financially. They disciple couples and send them into their calling. They bring people into their homes and show them God's love through their hospitality. They evangelize and make Christ known. And they nurture people on their faith journey.

Our culture tends to see the value of marriage through a selfish lens—how it benefits "me"—which is really a narcissistic way to look at it. In the world's view, the institution of marriage exists to make *your* life better, and your spouse is supposed to become the source of your happiness. The problem is, if you enter marriage with happiness or personal fulfillment as your primary motive, then you're sure to be disappointed, no matter how special your spouse might be. No other human can be solely responsible for your happiness.

Additionally, you're going to find yourself on an emotional roller coaster, as you constantly expect, or demand, that your spouse "fix" you. I'm not making excuses for neglectful or abusive spouses, but ultimately, only Christ can be the real source of love, joy, and fulfillment. That's why you need to pursue him as your first love while you're single, because then, once you're married, you will have a healthy source of joy and fulfillment based on true unconditional love rather than a source that's destined to fail sometimes.

Remember, you are not the center of the story. The union of husband and wife through marriage is a picture of the relationship between Christ and his church.

Just like God willed Christ and the church to become one body (Galatians 3:28, 1 Corinthians 12:23), so he willed for a man and woman to become one flesh in marriage (Genesis 2:24). It's no accident that marriage provides the language to explain Christ's relationship to the church (2 Corinthians 11:2) because the marriage of a man and woman is a copy and an image of the true marriage relationship.

As theologian Geoffrey Bromiley put it, "As God made man in His own image, so He made earthly marriage in the image of His own eternal marriage with His people."[1]

We need to view our marriages through the broader context of the love between God and humanity. Through daily acts of kindness, service, mutual love, and forgiveness, couples are called to imitate, however imperfectly, the unconditional love that Christ offers to the world.

God's Design for Your Marriage

The question each couple needs to wrestle with is, "Did you enter into this marriage as merely a legal transaction with the expectation that your spouse is responsible for your happiness and fulfillment?" This is a consumer mindset toward marriage. We sign the contract because of what we expect to receive from the other person.

But what if our marriage was based on God's broader context and his design for our relationships? What if we saw our relationship with our spouse as a picture of our relationship with Jesus Christ? What if our marriage was about the union of two souls in the deepest of friendships on a divine mission together?

At the beginning of his passage on marriage in Ephesians 5, before he talks about husbands loving their wives as Christ loves the church, Paul says, "Submit to one another out of reverence for Christ."[2]

This is how we establish true union as spouses. We submit to one another. What does this submission look like?

There have been times when my wife and I were 100 percent aligned from the beginning of a conversation about a decision we needed to make, especially some missional endeavor. When this happens, it's an awesome blessing, but most of the major decisions in our marriage have been challenging to work through. In some cases, we had seasons that lasted months where we weren't aligned about a decision. Even then, we were still submitting to one another.

A few years ago, the problem was a pending career decision. I thought God was calling me to start a coaching company at that time, though it would have required leaving the family business. Bobbi did not believe it was the right time—or the right thing to do. Any time we discussed it, she kept saying, "I'm not there yet."

For me, being an entrepreneur at heart, it was incredibly frustrating. When I get my mind fixed on something, I have a hard time slowing down. This led to a long, painful season of four or five months where my wife and I simply didn't see eye-to-eye on the issue.

The danger in these kinds of situations is that pride becomes magnified. I felt like my wife was controlling me, restraining me, even though I was the spiritual head of the household and God was clearly leading me down this path. As I told you, I'm really good at talking myself into stuff; however, the fact of the matter is, my wife was right, and I was wrong. I talked myself into something because I wanted it, but thank God, my wife's quiet, immovable spirit stayed anchored. She would not budge, and it kept me from making a big mistake.

It wasn't the right time. God kept me in the family business because his work through me in that place was not yet finished. Somehow, my wife knew it, even though she couldn't articulate it. She just knew, and every time I would bring it up, she would simply say again, "I'm not there yet."

In the end, we grew closer, and my respect and love for my wife became even deeper—especially after some time had passed, and I realized the importance of staying where I was for the season and purpose God had for me.

Being missional in your marriage doesn't mean that things are always wonderful, nor does it mean you always agree with one another. However, if you will submit to one another and act as a team, stay in the tough conversations and see them through to the end, and if you will pray together and be patient with one another until unity is reached, God will bless your marriage.

That's how you make him the center of all you do. To approach marriage as a mission, you must always come back to the center and meet Christ there. He alone will hold the marriage together, so if it feels like you're both farther from him, you are the ones who moved. You need to come back to him and get oriented correctly once again.

Missional Parents

Roughly twenty years ago, my wife and I took a vacation with her extended family to celebrate her grandparents' sixtieth wedding anniversary. Forty of us, including our aunt and uncle, Rod and Nancy Wildman, went to Punta Cana in the Dominican Republic. Rod and Nancy encouraged us to do something meaningful while we were "living it up."

As Rod put it, "I don't just want to go to a resort. Nancy and I both feel compelled to reach out to a local church so we can do something more."

He made some phone calls, talking to various people in the area where we were vacationing, and after several failed attempts to connect with local organizations, he finally met Pastor Borrell, who offered to show us a few areas in Punta Cana that most tourists never get to see.

Once we got to the resort, he escorted us to some of these nearby places, slums full of Haitian migrants who had been forced to reside there after coming to the Dominican Republic seeking better employment opportunities. We wound up bringing medicine and other vital supplies with us, along with treats and toys that our kids could hand out to local children. However, we soon realized that the children had other, greater needs.

Rod and Nancy were particularly heartbroken to learn that most children in the Dominican Republic have no access to school due to their poverty. As teachers themselves, they knew how vital a quality education is for a child if they're ever going to escape the cycle of poverty. On that trip, they were determined to find a way to do something about it.

Within a few years, Rod and Nancy had quit their jobs and started a ministry called 2nd Mile Missions that is dedicated to bringing a Christ-centered education to those impoverished communities. They launched that ministry fifteen years ago, and as of today, they have two schools with 1200 children being educated, from kindergarten all the way through high school. They've also established an orphanage for abused and abandoned girls, as well as several community projects that provide good-paying jobs and other opportunities for adults.

And all of that started on a family vacation. Think about that. A trip to celebrate my wife's grandparents' sixtieth wedding anniversary in Punta Cana turned into a ministry that went on to bless thousands. Amazing.

Intentional Parenting

This lesson stuck with me, and it has influenced how I view family vacations. Do we always do some kind of outreach while on vacation? No, in fact, we don't do it very often, but we find ways to combine fun and purpose when we can. However, the one thing we can do every time, on every trip, in every place is to have intentional conversations that keep God at the center of the story.

Every year, I take my boys on a "guys' trip," a tradition I started when my oldest son turned ten. Our first trip was a mountain biking excursion in the Manistee National Forest. We loaded our bikes with tents, supplies, and food and headed out on the Northern Trail. Every year since then, we've planned other adventures, but with each and every trip, I make it a point to sit around the campfire and talk about life and God. If possible, I combine the talk with some memorable object lesson.

When Malachi's younger brother, Levi, turned ten, I invited him to join us on our adventures. I found some rustic campsites near a larger reservoir a few hours south of our home. As I planned the trip, I thought and prayed about how I could make it purposeful—what kind of object lesson could I teach? Finally, I decided my sons and I would try to build a raft using only a hatchet, knife, and a bit of rope. Everything else had to come from the forest, including the logs.

Once the raft was complete, we would drift down the reservoir and have a wilderness adventure just like Huckleberry Finn. For the lesson, the raft would represent God, who is our "life raft" through the storms of this world. As we built the raft, it would represent our growing relationship with God. One piece at a time, we would drag logs from the forest down to the banks of the river (a time-consuming process) and create the raft, with each new piece representing another step in our faith journey. Eventually, we would have a raft that was strong enough and sturdy enough to get us through even the most turbulent waters.

What a beautiful picture! I could just imagine how our excitement and inspiration would grow as the all pieces came together.

Well, it turns out building a raft the Huck Finn way is a whole lot harder than I thought it would be! My sons and I labored, hunted, cut, dragged, and assembled that raft piece by piece all day long. As we worked, I attempted to create the metaphor that would make a lasting impact.

In the end, they remembered it alright, but not the way I intended.

Once we finally finished, we were excited to embrace the journey and set adrift on our crude little raft. My sons wobbled and teetered on the crude raft, trying hard to keep their balance, laughing and playing an adaptation of the game "King of the Mountain." I remember thinking, "This isn't quite how I thought this project would turn out."

We pushed off the shore on our great river adventure. We got about ten yards off shore when the current took us. I realized then that it might not be a good idea to set off on this voyage with no way back since our paddle looked like Moses's staff and only worked when it touched the ground. We poled our way back to shore, and that was the end of our journey. The whole adventure only lasted about ten minutes, but we went back to camp and made dinner around the campfire and laughed about our day.

The next morning a storm blew in, bringing fierce winds and a torrential downpour. We made the two-mile run back to our car and weathered the storm there. When we returned to the campsite after the storm, everything seemed just fine—until we walked to the water's edge and looked down at our little raft project from the day before. The storm had destroyed it! So much for my metaphor about building a solid foundation (maybe it should have been more of a Cortez lesson?). My big, purposeful trip was a bust.

I guess the only real moral of this story is, "Good luck, moms and dad." Make the most of your well-intentioned adventures, even when they don't go as planned. Isn't that what being missional is all about, anyway?

We focus so much on pursuing all that God has for us—being *on mission*—but sometimes the outcome isn't what we hoped for. Even so, we don't give up. We persevere and make every effort to finish the race that is marked out for us. This is especially true of parenting.

Caretaker, Cop, Coach, and Consultant

Look, parenting is hard. If you've got kids, I don't have to tell you that. It's *really* hard. I have four kids of my own who currently range in age from twelve to twenty-one. Bobbi and I have stumbled our way through the stages of parenting them: *caretaker*, *cop*, *coach*, and *consultant*. The role shifts from being physically demanding in the early stages to be mentally tough as you move toward adult parenting, but it's hard all along the way.

You might wind up with a kid whose personality is naturally kind, compliant, hard-working, and intelligent. However, even then, let's be honest, no child is completely void of challenges. Even the best child in the world is born with a sinful nature, and they're bound to struggle with temptations and trials throughout their childhood and into adulthood.

For most of us, our experience as parents is filled with a mix of great joy, fun, pleasure, and fulfillment but also challenge, heartbreak, frustration, and tough times. My wife and I have done our best to give our kids a solid foundation to build on, but that took a ton of work, mistakes, prayer, sleepless nights, faith, and continual pursuit of Jesus to show Bobbi and I how to raise them intentionally with a Biblical worldview.

We wanted to launch them into life in such a way that God would continue the good work he had planned for them. Without a solid foundation, it's so much harder for a young adult to continue following the Lord. Yes, it happens. God is able to lead someone even in the absence of a strong faith foundation, and I've seen him intervene in the lives of sinful, broken, lost souls who had no good earthly parents and bring even the most wayward souls to new life.

Most of the time, however, the strength of a young adult's faith comes down to the foundation we lay for them as parents. God will continue to build on that foundation as they mature into adulthood.

Still, we are all born with a sinful nature, and we discover this about our own children almost the minute we are given the privilege and responsibility of parenting them. An infant or toddler is at the center of their own story. They have no real concept of God yet. They learn quickly that they get what they want if they cry and scream. When they're awake, you're awake. They spend their days seeking to be fed, served, entertained, and grabbing at anything that interests them. Once you get close to the terrible twos, they also begin to assert their independence, and a fierce battle of will begins between parent and child.

As they continue to grow, your role as a parent shifts from caretaker to cop, as you constantly try to correct bad behavior, teach them right from wrong, safe from unsafe, nice from mean, and so on. The role shifts again as they enter their teen years, and you find yourself becoming more of a coach. Some things still need to be policed, boundaries set, penalties established for crossing those boundaries, and some boundaries even get lifted as the teen begins making their own decisions.

As a parent, it's tough to watch them deal with the negative outcomes of some of those decisions, and you might even feel tempted to become a "helicopter parent" to protect them from anything painful or uncomfortable. Sometimes, you feel like Jeremiah the prophet, warning them of imminent danger but then watching them blunder into that danger anyway. You just have to hope they'll learn the right lessons, even if they have to learn some of them the hard way.

Other times, you have to exercise authority as a parent and try to actively stop them from making a bad decision, which can become another battle of wills. But a battle of wills with a teenager is so much more intense and profound than a battle of wills with a two-year-old. Even though you're trying to help them, and want the best for them, they resent you for trying to control them and "not having a clue."

While parenting is filled with many blessings, joys, and lots of fun, the journey has some rough unpaved roads just like roads in Papua New Guinea. Somehow, you have to teach and show them what it means to make God the center of their world, and you have to do it in a way that won't discourage them or make them feel like their worth comes from not sinning (rather than from their inherent worth as a child of God). To make matters even more challenging, every child is different and requires a slightly different approach!

But the challenge doesn't stop when your kids become adults. You've been a caretaker, cop, and coach through their tumultuous teenage years, and now, as they enter adulthood, you move from coach to consultant. In some ways, this is the most difficult stage of parenting. To keep your relationship with your adult children strong, you have to stay out of the way, while still providing wisdom and advice when it's warranted (and wanted).

It's wonderful when adult children ask for advice, even more wonderful when they heed your advice and benefit from it, but it's painful when they disregard what you have to say and go down the wrong path—

a path you can see farther down than they can. As parents, we place so much pride in how our children turn out, so when a child rebels, we take it as a reflection upon our own parenting.

Relax a Little

I think we parents need to take a deep breath from time to time and relax a little. It'll be okay. We're not going to be perfect parents, and I'm not sure we should even strive to be. Let the grace of God flow through you as a parent. God has wise counsel for us in his word, he has a will for our lives, and his grace and mercy can cover our sincere mistakes. But we really need to rely on him as parents.

Too often, we try to raise our kids solely through our own strength, by our own wisdom. We think we know best, just like our teenage kids think *they* know best. Many of us place high expectations on our children. We assume they'll turn out perfect—not like all of those other kids who were raised wrong—but we ourselves know that we're far from perfect. How can imperfect people who depend so much on God's love and mercy expect their kids to be perfect?

Look at your own life. You're probably very familiar with your own sinful nature. You depend on God's forgiveness. Your kids will depend on his forgiveness, too. Nothing you do as a parent will protect them from having to deal with the reality of sin or the need for a savior. Nothing.

I've seen people raised in broken homes grow into God-fearing, high-impact ministers of the gospel, and I've seen people raised in good Christian homes go wayward, reject Jesus completely, and end up in jail or on the streets.

What's the point? Rather than setting expectations for how you think your kids *should* turn out, focus on building a solid foundation of faith, hope, and love so their trajectory is pointed toward Christ. Prepare the soil, plant the seeds, and water it. Then pray, pray, and pray that God makes it grow. That's being faithful to "training them in the way they should go" and trusting God to do the work in their hearts. And that's about all we can do.

Personally, I've found that the life we model consistently over a long period of time does more to establish a foundation than anything else.

What you teach your kids may have some impact, but what you model by the way you live becomes embedded into their character.

Yes, we should preach and teach, but I am guilty of preaching and teaching every single time there's any opportunity for it. Quite frankly, my kids get annoyed by it, which diminishes the impact. Sometimes, our kids just need to feel loved, not managed. And they definitely need to feel valued apart from their performance.

Being a missional parent means turning to the Word of God and bathing your parenting in prayer, making God the central focus of your family in how you raise, teach, discipline, and love your children. Your family begins with God, should be built on God, and ought to be shaped by God. Then commit to "training them in the way they should go so when they are old, they do not depart from it," but always with grace and dependence on God's help (Proverbs 22:6 ESV)[3].

Every child has different needs and responds uniquely to various parenting styles, so remain connected to the Holy Spirit and do your best to follow his prompting in conjunction with what the scriptures say. Friends, fellow parents, that's all we can do.

I can't tell you how many times I've been at a loss about what to do, crying out to God for help in handling a situation with one of my kids, and so many times, the Holy Spirit has eventually prompted some word or action from me that made all the difference. Parenting is a journey, just like our own spiritual walk, and it requires consistent, daily discipline over a long period of time. That's how character is developed and displayed, and that's what our children see in us. If my children retain one memory from growing up in my house, I want them to remember that God was the center of our family. Jesus was the priority, and our lives reflected our commitment to him.

Let me leave you with one final thought about being a missional parent. God intends for families to create a multigenerational legacy. I met my good friend and mentor Bill High through the consulting work he does for our family business. We first hired him to set up our business governance structure so it would have a lasting impact for generations to come. He is the leading expert in coaching families on how to establish a multi-generational family legacy.

During one of our sessions with him, he challenged us to create vision, mission, and values for our family and emphasized their importance in establishing a lasting family legacy. It's based on the premise of Deuteronomy 6:5-9 and Psalm 78:5-8.

> "Love the Lord your God with all your heart and with all your soul and with all your strength. These commandments that I give you today are to be on your hearts. Impress them on your children. Talk about them when you sit at home and when you walk along the road, when you lie down and when you get up. Tie them as symbols on your hands and bind them on your foreheads. Write them on the doorframes of your houses and on your gates" (Deut. 6:5-9 NIV)[4].

> "...He commanded our ancestors to teach them to their children, so the next generation might know them—even the children not yet born—and they in turn will teach their own children. So each generation should set its hope anew on God, not forgetting his glorious miracles and obeying his commands. Then they will not be like their ancestors—stubborn, rebellious, and unfaithful, refusing to give their hearts to God" (Psalm 78:5-8 NLT)[5].

This is why family vision, mission, and values are so important. There needs to be a central message for your family that embodies who you are and the Biblical values you live by. And if you want your great, great, great grandkids in a few hundred years to embrace and live a godly life, then that message needs to start *now* with your family, if it hasn't already been started by your parents.

When we do this, we give our kids the best chance at a life of following Jesus. Ultimately, each of your children will make their own decisions, but our job as parents is to prepare the soil and plant the seed so God can make it grow in his way and his mysterious timing.

Questions to Prayerfully Consider

- If you're single, have you considered the kind of impact God could have through you while you are single? Have you embraced this season of your life for his purposes?

- What if you had a missional mindset with your marriage? With your parenting? What might look different?

- Talk with your spouse about the idea of marriage as mission. Do you both feel you are aligned in purpose? Do you practice submitting to one another? Is Christ at the center or are you each anchored in your own interests?

- What are some things you could do to be more intentional or missional in the way you parent your children?

- Does your family have vision, mission, and values? If not, what might you do to make this a priority so you have a common language that can be passed down for generations?

- What if you made time to pray regularly with your spouse? With your children?

5

ALL IN FOR JESUS

J ennie began to feel ill, and soon realized she had come down with
another bout of amoebic dysentery. Her husband, Fitz, feared for her
life if they didn't get her medical attention, but it was the rainy
season. The risk of hiking out of the mountains during a monsoon to get
to a hospital in Burma seemed too dangerous. Even the surest-footed
Zaiwa and Lisu tribesmen avoided travel during the rainy season.

Rain in the rugged mountains of southwest China meant drenching
downpours making the steep rugged trails treacherous and impassable. If
the torrential rains that turned the trails and paths into slippery seas of
death weren't enough, the numerous leeches and mosquitos were sure to
suck the lifeblood from their victims.

Fitz and Jennie Fitzwilliam originally arrived in China in the fall of
1926 with China Inland Mission, and over a period of ten years God had
grown and stretched their faith in many ways. Despite their countless
trials and the challenges of living in extreme circumstances, they
continued to focus on their mission as sent ambassadors to the remote
tribes of Southern China. Would this latest trial halt the work of translating and delivering the gospel to the Lisu people?

It was a six-day journey down the steep mountain slopes to get to a
town where they could catch a train. Fitz and Jennie, as well as local
tribesmen, knew they had no choice but to carry her on a stretcher down

the mountain if they wanted to save her life. Either way, the risks were tremendous, but they trusted God to provide a way.

Reading their story today, I can't even comprehend that amount of faith. My son broke his ankle once playing in the backyard, and I treated it like a life-or-death situation as I rushed him to the ER. And it was only a twenty-minute drive! For most of us, when we deal with serious injury or illness, it takes minutes, maybe hours, to get help. So imagine if you had to struggle for days or weeks to get a very sick loved one to the hospital. If their life was on the line, and they were fading fast, how well would your faith hold up?

Jennie never forgot the dear Lisu men who bravely carried her through the downpours day after day, up and down one slippery trail after another. The trip was sheer misery, and with each passing day they became more discouraged, until finally they found themselves in the depths of despair. They couldn't comprehend God's purpose for this excruciating trial, and they began to wonder if he had forsaken them.

By the time they arrived at the American Baptist Hospital in Burma after a six-day hike and then a train ride from Lashio, Jennie was gravely ill. But God's work was not halted. In fact, this trial produced unforeseen fruit.

After months of recovery, God in his faithfulness used this time to provide the couple a way to finish the Zaiwa translation of Mark. Jennie later said, "It seemed like the end of the world when I was carried down on that cot to Burma, so deathly ill, but now I could see the Lord had this planned all along. God had brought good out of our desperation and trial."

Fitz and Jennie continued their work among the Lisu and Zaiwa, and many churches were born in these remote villages of China. Many people came to faith in Jesus. Then, another unexpected tragedy occurred. Fitz was teaching in a village a three-day hike from their home in Longchiu when he came down with a fever and grew very ill. He was determined to continue teaching, but he was forced to do so while laying on a cot.

Within a week, his fever worsened, he was unable to walk, and he finally collapsed. Attaching his cot to bamboo poles, several young Lisu took turns carrying him back to his home so he could be with Jennie, where he would hopefully recover.

When she saw him being carried into the village three days later, Jennie was shocked at his desperate condition. From there, they were able to summon a doctor, who came to the village on horseback. The doctor diagnosed Fitz with typhus and lung congestion. The doctor did all he could to help him, but in February of 1940 at the age of thirty-seven, Fitz died of typhus. The bottom fell out of Jennie's world. She was in shock and disbelief. She buried her husband in the mountains in Longchiu, near the village where they lived.

After Fitz's death, Jennie left the tribe seeking rest and recovery, but she fully intended to come back to Longchiu and continue the church plant work.

She traveled the long and difficult journey of several thousand miles from the southwestern mountains of China to the northeastern coast where Jack attended school. World War II was brewing at this time, and Japanese military forces had already invaded the country. Shortly after her arrival, on December 7, 1941, the Japanese attacked Pearl Harbor. War was on, and Jennie was unable to return to the tribe. She now had to deal with a new reality. The Chefoo School was located in a part of China that had been taken over by the Japanese in 1938. With Japan and the United States now at war, Jennie and Jack suddenly became enemy aliens, and they were considered prisoners of war.

At times their conditions were despicable, but they endured by faith, even as they prayed and longed for a safe return home to America. They would remain there until 1943 when a prisoner exchange was conducted between Japan and the US.

Finally, they were put on a ship, the *Gripsholm*, and sent home. After months and 21,000 miles of travel by sea, Jennie and a now-fourteen-year-old Jack arrived in Jersey City on December 1, 1943, where they were repatriated.

Sadly, even after the war in 1945, the rise of communism and the establishment of the People's Republic of China prevented Jennie from returning to her beloved Lisu and Zaiwa friends. She stayed in America for the rest of her life, but her zeal for the salvation of her friends put her on her knees in prayer for the next sixty years until she died in 2003.

As Jack climbed out of the van, he could hardly believe he had arrived. It had been sixty-two years since he'd left China with his mom during a prisoner exchange in 1943. After years of research, maps, and doing everything possible to locate Longchiu, his dream of finding the remote village where his parents had lived had finally come true.

Jack had longed to return to the village he'd grown up in, but he also hoped to locate his father's gravestone. He knew the gravestone had been moved from the original burial site to another part of the mountain, so the possibility of finding the exact location of Fitz's unmarked grave on this distant, remote mountain seemed close to impossible.

Eventually, not only did he find the burial site and gravestone, but he discovered something unbelievable—miraculous—in Longchiu. Despite the ravages of World War II, the rise of communism afterward, and Mao's Cultural Revolution, during which scores of Chinese people were tortured and killed and every form of religion condemned and banned, the church Jack's parents had planted seventy years earlier was alive!

When Jack visited the home of the local pastor, he saw a framed photo of his parents, Jennie and Fitz, and himself hanging on the wall, a photo taken in 1935. Pastor Pai made a broad sweeping motion toward the mountainside around them as he informed Jack that there were eighty Christian families living out there.

Amazingly, God was still at work in the mountains of southwest China because of the dedicated and committed men and women who blazed the trail long ago to reach the Lisu and Zaiwa people with the gospel. Pastor Pai and the Zaiwa believers were now carrying on this work.

This story is actually part of my family's legacy and heritage. You see, Fitz and Jennie are my wife's great grandparents, and Jack was her grandfather. My wife's grandmother, Alice, wrote a book documenting this journey called *A Legacy of Faith*. I encourage you to buy a copy and read it. It's an incredible story, and I have only shared a glimpse of the harrowing mission Fitz and Jennie set out on. They truly lived with wild abandon as missional leaders for what God had called them to. Because of their faithfulness to the mission of reaching Lisu and Zaiwa, they played a key role in changing the course of that community for generations. Today, nearly two-thirds of the Zaiwa people are Christian.

I've read their story multiple times, and each time I ask myself, "What if I lived life on mission with wild abandon like Fitz and Jennie? What does God want to do through me that has yet to be done? Are my inclinations toward comfort, abundance, and the pleasures of this world creating a filter that makes it harder for me to hear from God? Am I willing to receive his word with open hands and an open heart to serve him, whatever that might mean?"

Fitz and Jennie's story is an inspiration to me. It makes me wonder if I would rise up to the challenge and exhibit the kind of bravery they did, even if I was convinced of God's calling. They were all in, no holding back and no reservations.

What would that look like for you and me? As believers, what if we refused to live lukewarm lives any longer? What if we were all in for Jesus? What would change? How would lives be impacted? How might the hope of Christ be displayed to a hurting world? What if we lived life intentionally, purposefully, and missionally?

Western culture makes it so easy to live a lukewarm life. It's easy to blend in with other American Christians. Many of them don't look or live any differently than non-Christians, and plenty of churches have morphed into something that is entertaining on Sunday and leaves people feeling good without bothering or challenging them.

In 2 Timothy 4:3 NIV, Paul wrote a prophetic word about this: "The time will come when men will not put up with sound doctrine. Instead, to suit their own desires, they will gather around them a great number of teachers to say what their itching ears want to hear."[1] Does this describe church today? Some of us have become conditioned to expect easy self-help messages on Sunday rather than respond to the gospel and be changed.

In his book *The Spirit of the Discipline*, Dallas Willard writes, "This is an age for spiritual heroes—a time for men and women to be heroic in their faith and in spiritual character and power. The greatest danger to the Christian church today is that of pitching its message too low."[2]

The Dilemma of Following Jesus

From the beginning of Jesus' public ministry, he performed miracles as a sign of his authority, power, and glory. As people got healed, and other people witnessed these miracles, word quickly spread. Jesus became popular, and large crowds began to follow him. They were intrigued, and many of them wanted healing themselves.

Many in the crowds claimed to believe in him, and they were literally following him from place to place. Even so, we're told in John 2:25 ESV that "Jesus on his part did not entrust himself to them, because he knew all people."[3] What did Jesus see in the hearts of these people that kept him from committing himself to them?

He knew they were seeking signs and miracles, not a savior.

On another occasion, after Jesus fed 5,000 hungry people with five loaves and two fish, many of the people followed him. Again, he knew their hearts. He said, "You are seeking me not because you saw the signs but because you ate your fill of the loaves" (John 6:26 ESV)[4]. The crowd wanted another meal, but they failed to recognize Jesus as the "Bread of Life" (John 6:35).

As we continue the storyline through the Gospels, we see that as Jesus taught the crowds, he also sharpened his message toward the religious leaders of his day. In turn, some of them began to plot how they might kill him, which created a dilemma for many of his followers. The more he revealed himself as the Son of God, the more controversial his teaching became, and the more dangerous it became to follow him.

In fact, at one point, in John chapter 6, his teaching became so controversial that most of his followers turned back and stopped following him. When the Sanhedrin and officials arrested him and brought him to the Roman governor of Judea, the crowds were in uproar, demanding his death. Ultimately, this resulted in his flogging and a death sentence by crucifixion, which forced his followers into hiding, at least temporarily.

Now, considering Jesus' ministry, can you imagine if he were a pastor of a church today? If we follow the same basic storyline, you'd have a pastor who started small, then quickly became a megachurch pastor due to his message and miracles. In short order, his building would have been overflowing with people coming to see and hear him, and maybe experience the miracles for themselves.

However, over time, the intensity of his message, the controversy of some of his sermons, and the growing hostility from other religious leaders in the community, would begin to dampen the excitement over the miracles. People would accuse him of preaching "hard sermons." Others would become embarrassed or nervous about being associated with him. Some would say, "This guy is too much. I can't handle it."

One day, he would preach a sermon so difficult to accept that most people would leave the church right then and never return. A megachurch that once had lines out the door of people desperate to get inside, would now have empty pews, with just a small group of loyal church members still in attendance. All those who left would go looking for other churches with more comforting and encouraging sermons.

I wonder, would we consider that pastor a success? Or would he be subjected to public ridicule for his failure? Yet that's the Jesus we follow. Jesus wasn't about the numbers. He was about proclaiming the truth and power of the gospel. But the gospel is foolishness to the world. It offends because it pierces our pride, but those who truly, deeply respond to the message are radically transformed.

Here are some challenging questions that I think churches of all sizes should consider: Why are people entering your church doors? Do they desire to know the Savior? Are they trying to unpack what it means to follow him? Are we teaching who he is and letting the power of the gospel transform hearts, producing a fully devoted response, as people rejoice about who he is and what he has done for us? Are we equipping them to be missional in life, to go out as ambassadors of Christ? Are the pastors focused on teaching the word as it is, even when it doesn't feel all that great to listeners?

Or are the crowds growing because we soften the impact of the gospel, take the edge off Jesus' teaching, and give them a half-baked truth that's easier to digest? Are the pastors trying to entertain people and be liked, or are we preaching the gospel even though it may turn some people away?

If Jesus was the pastor of your church, how different would things be? What would change?

There's a broken world out there! Half the world lives on less than $2 a day. In the first world, our pet cats and dogs eat better and live better than most people in the third world. And consider these bleak statistics: Every ten seconds, a child dies of a hunger-related cause. Every twenty-one seconds, a child dies of a waterborne disease. One in eight people world-wide (over 800 million) go hungry every day, and over 700 million people do not have access to clean water. Every week, hundreds of thousands are trafficked around the world for human sexual exploitation.

In regard to our faith, thousands of our brothers and sisters around the world face imprisonment and persecution. Even so, there are still a billion people who haven't even heard the name of Jesus.[5] While progress is being made on many fronts, there is still much work to do and a lot at stake.

I could go on and on about the injustices in the world. What are we, the church, going to do about it? I read an anonymous quote once that really convicted me and has stuck with me:

"Sometimes I would like to ask God why he allows poverty, suffering, and injustice when he could do something about it."

"Well then, why don't you ask him?"

"Because I am afraid he would ask me the same question."

What are we doing about it? Statistics show that only 18 percent of pastors place helping the poor as a priority. While the total income of American churchgoers is over $6.5 trillion, the average Christian gives only 2 percent. If American churchgoers simply applied the 10 percent tithing principle, it would produce $500 billion more that would be available to fund serving the poor and seeing the gospel expanded to the ends of the earth. Americans overall spend twice as much on elective cosmetic surgery than the total income for overseas ministry, five times as much on lottery tickets, and more than ten times that on household pets! These statistics are shocking and illustrate the nature and focus of our culture. Jesus tells us that where our heart is so will our treasure be. The imbalance of how we allocate resources and spend our time is distracting us from the purpose of which we have been created. A discerning quote by Ralph D. Winter alludes to this: "Obedience to the great commission has more consistently been poisoned by affluence than anything else."[6]

Reflect on that quote in light of the following scriptures: 1 Timothy 6:6-10, 17-19, Matthew 6:24, 19:21, Luke 16:13-15.

It's easy to be comfortable, enjoy life, and relegate the commands of Jesus to serve the poor, take care of the orphans and widows, spread the gospel, and risk everything to follow him to the back of our minds. Someone else will do all of that, right? So we push away the hard teachings, the uncomfortable things. No one wants pain, no one wants suffering and persecution and challenge and danger.

Instead, we retreat. We retreat to comfort. We retreat to living for ourselves and a half-hearted living for Jesus, embracing only the parts of what he says that make sense and don't push us too far out of our comfort zone. We live lukewarm. We live like the Laodiceans.

David Platt gave a powerful sermon around this. Here is an excerpt:

"With the mammoth needs of a world without Christ in front of us...we can retreat from this mission into a land of religious formalism and wasted opportunity, or [like Fitz and Jennie] we can risk everything to fulfill the divine purpose for which we have been created, and I say let's risk it all. For the sake of a billion people who haven't heard his name, I say let's risk it all. For the sake of millions in our country who are heading to a Christless eternity, I say let's risk it all. For the sake of the lost people you and I know, and our families, and our neighborhoods, and our communities, let's risk it all. For the sake of our lives, our families, our churches, our children's lives, let's risk it all...Are we going to die in our religion? Or are we going to die in our devotion?"[7]

Following Jesus may lead us to places we wouldn't naturally choose, places that are dirty, dangerous, far from home, or uncomfortable, but we follow Jesus into these places because we believe he is worth it. We believe in what he has done for us, and our response is that of devout service in humility and adoration for his grace and love. We believe he has given us a meaningful purpose in his story of redeeming people to himself.

Are we all in with our money, our time, our priorities, with our entire lives? I invite you to join me in this journey of unpacking what that looks like. Let us go before God each day with this larger view of purpose in mind, with our compass pointing toward True North, and he will without a doubt direct our steps.

Sometimes that means staying right where you are. Perhaps that's how you feel led, or perhaps you're not feeling led at all even though you want something different. Sometimes he directs us to take one small step at a time, with one small task, one conversation, one smile, one kind word.

Sometimes we're called to take a giant leap of faith to the ends of earth, and God is beckoning some to go into hard places.

Years ago, I heard about a mega-church in Southern California that had an opening for a pastor. They received over 1,000 applications. At the time, we were living in Papua New Guinea. I knew of several tribes who had heard about missionaries coming in to share "Tok bilong God" (God's Talk). I read letters from the tribal leaders requesting missionaries to come live with them so they could hear this story about God. They, too, had an opening for a pastor who would bring them the Good News.

How many applicants do you think the tribal leaders in Papua New Guinea got? Zero. None. The mission agency had to raise up more missionaries to bring them God's story.

It doesn't make sense for God to call 1,000 equipped believers to pastor an established mega-church but call no one to pastor a church in the jungle, especially when scriptures says that all nations must hear the gospel and then the end will come (and that in heaven, every tribe, tongue, and nation will gather around the throne). Jesus has revealed the mystery of his mission, but who will listen to his call and respond in obedience?

I have said that the "what" and "where" are irrelevant because living on mission transcends what we do. And while that is Biblically true, we must also recognize that there is an unmet need for expanding the gospel among the nations. Taking the gospel to the ends of the earth is an imperative in scripture. Jesus says the laborers in the field are few so we should pray that the Lord will send out workers into his harvest (Matthew 9:37-38).

All Christians should assume this call and inquire of the Lord what kind of work he would have us do. If we are all in, we should be able to say to the Lord, "Whatever, wherever, whenever, whatever the cost."

Are we all in for that?

Yes, we will stumble together, lift each other up when we need it, speak hard truth when needed, and experience community as broken vessels in need of God's grace as we strive to finish the race that he has marked out for us. Join me in considering, praying, and pursuing a life on mission that is all in for Jesus!

Questions to Prayerfully Consider

- What if Jesus was the pastor of your church? What would look different?

- What if you went all in for Jesus? What would look different?

- What if God is calling you to something difficult or a hard place? Would you go? Do you believe it would be worth it?

- Have you come to the point in your faith journey where you can honestly say, "Lord, here I am! Send me. Whatever, wherever, whenever, whatever the cost?" If not, how might you approach God in your prayer life?

- Are you all in with your finances? Whose money is it and how is it being stewarded?

6

WHAT IF THE GOOD NEWS WAS REALLY GOOD NEWS?

My interest in music started as a young child. According to my mother, even though I didn't know the notes, I would often create masterpieces on the piano by simply stringing together sounds into something that was pleasing to the ear. Well, she may have exaggerated in calling them "masterpieces," but I certainly showed some indication of a natural affinity for music early on.

There's the old child prodigy story where a young boy finds a beat-up acoustic guitar with only two strings in his grandma's closet, picks it up out of curiosity, and discovers that he's a guitar prodigy. The first part of that story happened to me. The second part, not quite. I found the guitar when I was twelve, and I did have an ear for music.

My grandma's neighbor, Ray Earl, was an old-time folk recording artist (but who wouldn't be with a name like Ray Earl?). When I found an old K guitar with two strings, I took it to Mr. Earl's house, and he strung it up for me and taught me two songs: "House of The Rising Sun" and a 12-bar blues progression in E. I developed an appetite to learn and become like Ray (except for the bib overalls, banjo belly, and flannel shirt).

I was intrigued with finger picking and started to learn patterns. I'd discovered John Denver and thought his finger picking was super clean, so I began following along to the fingerpicking songs on his greatest hits album. Gradually, I became a decent guitar player.

In April of 1994, my freshman year of high school, I was invited on a ski trip to the beautiful Rocky Mountains of Colorado by my good friend Josh Wildman (who would become a family business partner six years later, a partnership that has lasted for over two decades). Josh was a few years older than me, but we competed on the high school swim team together and became buddies. I also happened to have a crush on his younger sister Bobbi who was my age. Bobbi and I had a developing friendship during our freshmen year, and as the friendship grew, I shifted from hanging out with Josh to hanging out with Bobbi—more on that story later.

I had never been to Colorado before, and I'd only skied a few times. Josh's dad, Brent Wildman, had been leading ski trips for fifteen years. Brent and a few adult volunteers would take fifty to eighty high school kids, pack them in vans, and drive to Winter Park, Colorado for four amazing days of skiing and snowboarding. But these trips were about more than just skiing. In fact, skiing was merely the attraction to get people out into God's creation where they would feel invigorated and challenged both physically and, more importantly, spiritually. It gave Brent and the other adults an opportunity to share the gospel with some adventurous teens.

As we headed out of the west side of Denver on Interstate 70, someone suggested we crank up some John Denver in the van. Since I was a big fan of his, I knew most of the lyrics, so I sang along. It was an inspiring moment, attempting to mimic this singer I'd listened to and learned from as we drove through the very mountains he often sang about.

Actually, Brent reminded me of John Denver in many ways. He had similar hair and the same warm smile that made guests feel welcome. He always had friends, guests, and acquaintances coming and going at his house, and I was one of those lucky people.

When his daughter and I started dating, we had the honor (and embarrassment) of being crowned prom king and queen, and then we went off to college in Tennessee. During the first year of college, I went to Brent and asked his permission to marry his daughter. He was happy to give his blessing, and I ran with it. Bobbi and I got married right after we had both turned twenty.

I've known Brent Wildman now for thirty-three years, and I've acquired enough stories to write a trilogy of books about him. But one thing stands far above everything else: his heart for evangelism and sharing the gospel. He has modeled for us what it looks like to live and act as if the Good News really were good news. His life revolves around people, relationships, and making Christ known everywhere he goes. Whether in a business setting, during an early morning group swim or bike ride, on an adventure trip, during Sunday lunch with family, on a marriage retreat, or with random people, he strives to make Christ known.

On multiple occasions, I've been with Brent someplace, in the middle of some activity, when he suddenly disappears. Someone would say, "Hey, where's Brent?" At first, we would be irritated, because we always seem to be waiting on him. But that irritation quickly turns to conviction when we find that he's off doing the Lord's work—acting like the Good News is good news.

We'll be getting gas at a gas station, and I'll look over and see him building a relationship with some stranger on the other side of the pump. Then he'll ask them about their faith. Or we'll be sitting in a restaurant, and Brent will excuse himself to use the restroom. He'll be gone for fifteen minutes, and when we finally check on him, we'll find that he stopped on the way and started chatting with a stranger.

Or on a bike ride together, we'll stop for a quick break, and suddenly he'll strike up a conversation with a young couple selling stuff out of the back of their car. He's genuinely interested in buying something, yes, but he's also investing into them and making a positive impact. Meanwhile, the rest of us are impatiently waiting to get rolling again.

Whether we're in the grocery store, at a coffee shop, at lunch, or on a road trip, you always find yourself waiting for Brent because at some point he's going to break your routine to live like Jesus.

And that brings us back to that life-changing ski trip to Winter Park when I was fourteen years old. I had not yet put my faith in Jesus as Lord and Savior. I'd heard about God, and I'd been to church, but I didn't yet understand how my brokenness and sinfulness could all be wiped away by a loving God who sent his son to take the penalty of my sin.

I only went on the trip because my buddy invited me, and I wanted to go skiing with him. I had no idea that my whole life was about to change.

Every evening we had regular meetings during which Brent would share an intentional and purposeful story, and each night those stories built up toward his final talk, during which he shared the Good News. He then challenged his attentive young listeners to consider where their hope lay and extended an invitation for them to put their faith in Jesus.

I was one of the broken souls in need of a savior, so after the meeting, I approached Brent. He walked me through the gospel and then prayed with me as I accepted the work of Jesus on my behalf. I was born again at that moment! It's crazy to think that I was brought to salvation by the man who, unbeknownst to me, would later become my father-in-law.

We Speak What We Love

I attended that ski trip every spring break for the rest of high school, and my wife and I continued to attend occasionally over the years. Once our children were old enough, we started going every year as a family. Last year, Brent celebrated his forty-fifth year of leading those ski trips. Amazing. Many have come to the Lord on these trips, and I'm one of them.

I love Colorado, John Denver, and the 2nd Mile Ski Trip. Since that first trip, it has become a tradition to blast John Denver songs as we drive out of Denver and head to Winter Park. I will continue to shamelessly promote these trips so we can continue to minister to a lot of young people each year.

But that's what we all do, don't we? We talk about and promote things we love. We share our great experiences because we want other people to experience them, too. I often feel challenged when I consider whether or not I'm as passionate about sharing the Good News of Jesus as I am the other things I love in life.

If the words that come out of our mouths reflect what's in our hearts and what we treasure, then shouldn't we be eager to share the gospel? That's certainly true of Brent. He talks about the things he loves, and he has a lot of passions and interests. He's an adventurous guy, but he talks about the Good News at least as much as anything else. His heart is overwhelmed with God's love so much that it can't be contained. It spills out in every area of his life.

So what's in our heart? What overflows from your heart into your thoughts, conversations, and relationships?

Matthew 12:34-40 NIV gives us a perspective on this, and words of caution.

"Make a tree good and its fruit will be good, or make a tree bad and its fruit will be bad, for a tree is recognized by its fruit. You brood of vipers! How can you speak good, when you are evil? For out of the abundance of the heart the mouth speaks. The good person out of his good treasure brings forth good, and the evil person out of his evil treasures brings forth evil. I tell you, on the day of judgment people will give account for every careless word they speak for by your words you will be justified and by your words you will be condemned."[1]

It seems Jesus doesn't take this topic lightly. Neither should we. We should feel challenged to adopt the same mindset as Paul: "For I am not ashamed of the gospel, for it is the power of God for salvation to everyone who believes" (Romans 1:16 ESV)[2].

So, what if we acted, spoke, and lived like we truly believed that the Good News is good news? Would we share it more? What would change about the way we treat others? Would we create more opportunities to share the gospel through word and deed with others? How would it change the way we parent? How would it change the way we treat our spouse? Neighbors? Strangers?

And how would it change the way we run our businesses and treat our employees?

Questions to Prayerfully Consider

- What if you lived and acted like the Good News was really good news? What would look different?

- Do you feel God has given you a spirit of power, love and self discipline and not one of timidity? If you believe this truth, how might it impact your intentionality with sharing the Good News?

- How might it impact your confidence in sharing your personal story and testimony to others, highlighting the impact of the Good News on your life?

- Have you considered what it means to you when Jesus says that the overflow of the heart is what the mouth speaks? What do you find yourself speaking about most? It's likely a regurgitation of whatever you're feeding yourself.

PART II

LEADING MISSIONALLY

7

GOD IN YOUR DAY JOB

A good friend of mine, Riley Fuller, is the founder of an organization called Humanity & Hope United that focuses on sustainable change in "forgotten" communities in rural Honduras. They define hope as "the belief that the best is yet to come, plus action that makes those beliefs likely to come true." Their mission is to listen first, then empower people through self-directed, sustainable change in six key areas: infrastructure, economy, community, health, education, and leadership.

Riley is an awesome friend to many, also a father, husband, and follower of Jesus. God is using him and his nonprofit to impact lives for generations.

I first visited Honduras in 2006, on a short-term mission trip with my wife and a few others, including Riley's parents. My wife and I connected with them and enjoyed their company, including their kids who were in their late teens. Normally, they were a family of five, but one of their older kids was missing on that trip. Surprisingly, it was Riley. You see, Riley had refused to go to Honduras with his family because he wanted nothing to do with God.

He stayed at home indulging in his unhealthy appetites, which included wrecking his father's car. I'd never met Riley, but his brothers and parents were great people. It was hard for me to imagine that they had a wayward son back home causing trouble.

The following year, in 2007, Riley finally arrived in Honduras, but only because they forced him to go for wrecking the car the previous year. As Riley describes it now, "Before that first trip to Honduras, I knew nothing about putting myself in someone else's shoes. I was blind and selfish. I had no idea how much struggle and heartache happened throughout the world, and I didn't know how much human potential was being wasted. I also didn't know how much we could do to change it if we worked together."

Stepping off the bus for the first time, Riley saw a crude house covered in a plastic tarp to keep the rain out. Printed on the tarp were the words, "Delta Trash." That moment changed everything for Riley. Here was a family facing not only food deprivation, dirty water, high local crime, education ending in the sixth grade, and an income of less than $2 per day —they also lived in a house literally labeling them "trash."

Riley says, "None of it made sense to me, and I became furious. I had no idea why I had won the birth lottery, but I knew I had to use what I'd been given to help people who were suffering."

It set him on a new life trajectory. In fact, Riley started Humanity & Hope United as a direct result of the injustice he experienced on that trip. Even though he didn't know or follow God yet, something inside of him called him to become a solution for those suffering people. Years later, he would realize that the source of those feelings was rooted in God's love for him and the people he was there to serve. Jesus is now a central part of who he is, the source of his love, and an outcome of the work they are doing.

Different Cultures, Universal Needs

Sometimes the connections of God come full circle. Riley's story is a perfect example. Nine years after my first trip to Honduras with the Fuller family (except Riley), he asked me to join the board of his nonprofit so I could focus on integrating spirituality into the work they do. H&H now works with local pastors to incorporate preaching the gospel into the villages they serve. The humanitarian work has become a vessel through which the light of Christ shines. I served on their board for six years and made many trips with Riley to support their work.

One of the things that makes this organization so special is the heart behind it. From the beginning, as they conduct village assessments to determine how to help, they start with questions. They don't impose an assumed fix with an ethnocentric mindset; instead, they ask locals what would be meaningful to them. They get to know them, build relationships, ask about their desires, and learn what would make life better.

The Hondurans in these rural communities have a different worldview and a different lens through which they look at life, a perspective that Americans struggle to comprehend or relate to. Their culture is unique and special to them. Riley and the team respect those cultural differences and truly want to help in whatever way is most meaningful to them.

One of the topics I studied and taught as a missionary overseas was the "Eight Universals of Culture." These universal principles provide a grid through which missionaries are able to understand thought patterns and expressions of people they minister to, which helps them effectively communicate within their context and ultimately present the gospel in a way that's relative to the culture.

In other words, societies living in different environments around the world have the same basic needs. Anthropologists classify these needs categorically under these eight culture "universals."

Honduras is very different from the US, but their distinct cultural approach to doing things still leads to fulfilling the same basic human needs as every other culture on the planet. For the most part, culture is neither right nor wrong, just different ways through which a group of people expresses themselves and meets their basic human needs.

So, when Riley's nonprofit asks the Hondurans what they need, their first answer is usually "work." Above all, they want work. That came before clean water, food, electricity, or any other need.

They still needed and wanted those other things, and eventually those needs were met, but work was consistently at the top of their list. On some level, people in every culture want to be productive, to be caretakers, to create things of value. As I've lived and traveled to countries all over the world, I've seen this need in Central America, Africa, the South Pacific, China, and more. The cultures are different, but work is one of those universal needs.

Why is this? Because there is dignity in work. People need work to thrive emotionally, physically, and spiritually. Without it, they feel emptiness.

As Timothy Keller writes,

"Work has dignity because it is something that God does and because we do it in God's place, as his representatives. We learn not only that work has dignity in itself, but also that all kinds of work have dignity." He goes on to say, "All work has dignity because it reflects God's image in us, and also because the material creation we are called to care for is good."[1]

It's also a catalyst for forward progress. Once the mothers in Honduras started working, they began to feel more of God's power in their lives and began making healthier decisions for their families. Kids became healthier and went to school longer, and homes became places where both parents could serve as examples of God's power to provide and create goodness. Parents working, and the resulting empowerment, gave their kids a sense of dignity and hope for the future.

The longing for work is hard-wired in us. It was established from the beginning of creation that we are to work, take care of our world and one another, and contribute to society in some meaningful way.

Americans have this same need, too. However, we have systems in place that have watered down this basic human need. For example, the current economic climate in America has created more jobs than there are workers to fill them, so unlike in many countries, we have choices. Also, the government has created programs to take care of people, which is a good thing, but in some cases, this has also created reasons for people not to work.

In Honduras, people want to work and truly need it, not only to meet physical needs but also their emotional, social, and psychological needs as well. In many cases, they don't have any real choices because there is little work outside of subsistence living.

Often, people in America can survive without working, at least on a basic level. But what if we don't work? What if we choose to not contribute, to live off others even when we have the ability to work? Well, Gallup has a few things to say about that: "About one in five Americans who have been unemployed for a year or more say they currently have or are being treated for depression—almost double the rate among those who have been unemployed for five weeks or less."[2]

Gallup finds that "unemployed Americans are more than twice as likely as those with full-time jobs to say they currently have or are being treated for depression." Gallup also says, "Psychologists have long associated unemployment with a variety of psychological ailments, including depression, anxiety, and low self-esteem."

That sounds a lot like how the Hondurans felt before they had work! It's universal in the culture: people need work to be healthy mentally, emotionally, and psychologically.

God's View of Work

What does God say about work? We'll look at what God says in His word, but I would like to encourage you to explore this topic deeper. There are some great resources out there that dig into this topic of work from a Biblical viewpoint, including the websites *Answers in Genesis* and *Theology of Work*. A few great books are Timothy Keller's *Every Good Endeavor*, and Erik Cooper's *Missional Marketplace*.

First, let's create a healthy working definition of work. If we look at scripture, we can see how God worked: creating, planting a garden, providing, and becoming a caretaker. You see Adam and Eve were given dominion over the earth, commanded to be fruitful and care for the land and animals.

As we move throughout the Old Testament, we see all kinds of work being done. Prophets, teachers, servants, mothers, politicians, and manufacturing. Jesus himself was a carpenter, teacher, and leader. He did both business and ministry. The Apostle Paul made tents, though his primary vocation was a missionary.

What Is Work?

How can we define what we mean by "work?" There are many relevant ways to define it, so instead of choosing one, I'll use a summarized definition of work through a Biblical lens. From that perspective, we can say "work" is physical or mental energy that, by God's sovereignty, is used to sustain life, create culture, and serve society for the common good. To put it more practically, work is the energy spent on anything that serves humankind and God's purposes, including the work done by both believers and non-believers as viewed through the lens of the Doctrine of Common Grace.

From a Christian worldview, God has called everyone to follow Christ and participate in his redemptive work, and we have all been commissioned as his ambassadors. God has also commanded that we work for six days and rest on the seventh day. We know from scripture that some are called into ministry, like Paul, some are anointed as leaders, such as Nehemiah or the many kings that ruled over Israel and Judea, and some are called to what might seem like less meaningful jobs from the world's perspective.

If Peter calls all believers saints, and Paul calls all believers ambassadors, then there is no hierarchical spiritual value placed on the specific work. Some work may have a more noticeable impact on society, but that doesn't necessarily mean it's any more noble from a spiritual standpoint. In the book of Romans, humanity is pictured as clay: dirty, marred, and full of flaws. God, at his own discretion, chooses to form lumps of clay for different purposes, some "for special purposes and some for common use."[3]

God ordered the world and set certain laws in motion to make our existence possible. For example, he made night and day. What if it was only dark and there was no sun? He made the law of gravity. What if we were just floating in the darkness of outer space? These are laws we humans have little control over. They are ordered and controlled by God.

There are laws of physics, chemistry, biogenesis, the ecosystem, planetary motion, mathematics, and much more. The most fundamental laws of nature exist only because God wills them, and he uses them to sustain the universe. Consider Colossians 1:16-17 ESV:

"For by him all things were created, in heaven and on earth, visible and invisible, whether thrones or dominions or rulers or authorities—all things were created through him and for him. And he is before all things, and in him all things hold together."[4]

In the order of creation, God created human beings and gave them dominion over the earth. When we take that dominion into our various spheres of influence, chaos is put to order. Imagine how it would be if we didn't have some people who can design and construct buildings and other people who keep them clean. If we didn't have some people who design and manufacture trash cans, and other people who empty the trash out of them. If we didn't have some people who make and package food, and others who sell the packaged food at the store. Some who design and manufacture toilets, and others who empty septic systems.

Everything around us has been designed and built by human hands applying the laws of physics that God ordered. If people didn't work, we wouldn't have any of our basic needs supplied, and that requires all kinds of different people doing all kinds of different tasks—not just for civilization to function, but for our very survival.

John Calvin had this to say about work:

"We know that people were created for the express purpose of being employed in labor of various kinds, and that no sacrifice is more pleasing to God than when every person applies diligently to his or her own calling, and endeavors to live in such a manner as to contribute to the general advantage."[5]

So if this is the case, then all work must honor God. That seems to be what Calvin thought. Of course, as with anything, your work only honors God if you do the work as if you were doing it for Him, not for people. Colossians 3:17 says, "Whatever you do, whether in word or deed, do it all in the name of the Lord Jesus, giving thanks to God the Father through him."[6]

Through work, we take dominion in some small way and bring order, but if we do it in the name of Jesus, then we see a higher purpose in even the most mundane task. Consider what the following verses have to say about this topic:

- **Proverbs 13:4 ESV**, "The soul of the sluggard craves and gets nothing, while the soul of the diligent is richly supplied."[7]

- **Ephesians 4:28 ESV,** "Let the thief no longer steal, but rather let him labor, doing honest work with his own hands, so that he may have something to share with anyone in need."[8]
- **1 Thessalonians 4:11–12 ESV,** "And to aspire to live quietly, and to mind your own affairs, and to work with your hands, as we instructed you, so that you may walk properly before outsiders and be dependent on no one."[9]
- **2 Thessalonians 3:10 ESV,** "For even when we were with you, we would give you this command: If anyone is not willing to work, let him not eat."[10]

So, the theological idea I am presenting is that there are certain universal laws that God put into place. If we are called to work, take care of, or produce something of value, if we are also called to be missional as commissioned ambassadors for Christ, and if we assume we are to live integrated lives, then the outcome would look something like this:

work + mission = obedience, meaning, and fulfillment.

The problem: If there is a divine purpose in our work, then what creates the sacred and secular divide in our lives? Why don't Christians see eternal value in their day jobs? Why do we compartmentalize work and mission?

I believe we create our own sacred and secular divide. It's an individual choice, not a culturally forced perspective. We go to church, we go to work, we go to a football game, we go to a grocery store, we go on a mission trip, we go to a prayer meeting, and we go to a bar. In each context, most of us function with certain presuppositions about our mindset and how we are to act in each of those places. However, it seems we should instead maintain a sense that we are fully integrated physical and spiritual beings in every context, and that reality transcends the place we're at or what we're doing.

Unfortunately, too many Christians lack an understanding of Biblical theology in regard to God's unfolding revelation throughout scriptures, which culminates in the revelation of his full glory of Christ. If we don't understand God's redemption story, we will struggle to understand how we fit into it in a meaningful way.

The solution: I run the risk of oversimplifying this, but I genuinely believe it's quite simple. I believe we need to focus on Jesus and make time to build a relationship with him, know him, and understand what his word says. We are not the center of the story; Jesus is. However, we are human *beings*, and our "being" transcends our "doing," which paradoxically produces a proper outcome of doing, and that's how we honor God. In other words, in all the work we do in every part of our lives, we can and do bring glory to God.

Here's a story about what can happen when we do this.

The Story of Brother Lawrence

In the 17th century, Brother Lawrence was a servant in a monastic community for fifty years. His story has been an inspiration for me, and eliminates any excuse I might have for not adopting a prayerful attitude of honoring God in my work.

What was so special about Brother Lawrence? He learned how to practice the presence of God and displayed humility in every situation. He never became a priest but remained a lay monk, and for years his main duty was cooking and cleaning the kitchens of the priory. When his health began to fail, Brother Lawrence was given the responsibility of repairing sandals for the monks.

His jobs were not glamorous, they were the lowest of the low, yet his life had an incredible impact on many people, even hundreds of years after his death.

He wrote:

"We ought not to be weary of doing little things for the love of God, who regards not the greatness of the work, but the love with which it is performed. And it is not necessary to have great things to do. I turn my little omelet in the pan for the love of God."[11]

Despite Lawrence's lowly position, lack of education, and simple language, he became increasingly valued over the years for his spiritual wisdom and the peace he showed. He was sought after by those who knew of him, but it wasn't until after he passed away that a book was created from a collection of his writings.

Over time, Brother Lawrence's down-to-earth sayings about the spiritual life became prized; an estimated 22 million copies of his book have been printed in English alone! If you want a humbling read that will inspire you to go deep in your faith, daily disciplines, and relationship with God, check out the book *Practicing the Presence of God* by Brother Lawrence.

What if Brother Lawrence had thought his work was meaningless and mundane? His choice to honor God with his work and a focus on his presence all day has impacted millions of people, but he was just a guy working in a monastery doing menial, mundane tasks. He was not famous during his lifetime. In fact, he was hardly known until later in his life and not widely read until many years after his death. It's incredible to me. I want to be like Brother Lawrence when I grow up!

Do some jobs stink? Yes, they do. Some jobs *literally* stink. It's nice to find a job you're good at, that isn't miserable, but whatever the work is, your mindset should be the same. If you're called to some greater work, pursue it, but you can honor God with whatever you're doing in the meantime. You do so by having a missional mindset about your work, a heart that stays close to God, and communing with him daily.

When you do that, God will give you the strength and fruit of the Spirit you need each day at work. If you long for greater work, he may eventually give you a vision or plant a seed that could lead you somewhere else. But until then, you can still honor him right now, whether you're selling insurance, sweeping floors, or flipping burgers. The *what, where,* and *how* don't matter. All that matters is *who* you're serving and *why*.

When you have a missional mindset, you become part of creating an amazing workplace culture wherever you are! What if you made the choice to honor God in your work by making someone's day better? What if you made the choice to prepare the soil, plant the seed, or water the plant by allowing the light of Christ to shine through you? Imagine how much more fulfilling and purposeful your job would become!

You can start doing that now. Go before the Lord tomorrow morning and ask him to show you how. Make a commitment to live and work for him, then seek opportunities in the workplace.

Sounds easy enough, doesn't it? Yes, it's simple in concept, but it's also a journey of learning to be consistent over time. Expect it to be tough. Expect that sometimes you'll feel like it's not worth the effort. I have served in many different roles in both the business world and on the mission field. Some I liked more than others. Sometimes it was all I could do to muster up the courage to face the day and put on the mindset of Christ. And there were seasons when I failed miserably at this, as I complained and groaned constantly.

I learned a lesson while on the mission field in Papua New Guinea. As I was struggling through some challenges, I felt like God spoke to me and said, "You don't have to enjoy something to do it with joy." Even though some things were unpleasant, I could choose to have a spirit of joy because I knew I was working for a bigger purpose and playing a role as a commissioned ambassador in God's story.

There are days where joy will slip, but don't let discouragement be the enemy within. Each morning, we have an opportunity to once again surrender our day to God and serve him in whatever capacity he has us in for that season. Jesus commands us to pick up our cross and follow him daily. Carrying a cross is no easy feat, and each day we have to muster up the courage to pick it up again, and again, and again. It's a daily choice to have a missional mindset that most certainly includes our work.

To close out this chapter, I am going to get really vulnerable for a moment and share a few excerpts from my prayer journal from over ten years ago. I want to give you a glimpse of my own journey as I wrestled through this issue of "work." These journals were written at a time when I was coming back into the business world after having lived on the mission field for three years.

8/18/13 – What does this look like? I don't know. I have often pondered how Jesus would live and work in this society and culture. What type of job would he have? How would he live that out? What type of home would he have? In some ways, I have concluded that the "what" isn't nearly as important as *how* he lived it out. He walked with the Father and did as the Father said. His work, position, home, etc. were irrelevant. But how he lived it out was very different from how the world says to live it out.

I often reflect on John 13, when Jesus washes the disciples' feet. This combined with a quote from J. Oswald Sanders, "Greatness comes only by way of servanthood, and first place in leadership is gained only by becoming everybody's slave." Business is the means for me. It's the vessel in which God will work through me to reach people in this community and out in the world. I must continue to focus on walking with the Father, listening to the Holy Spirit, loving others, and ultimately to being a servant of all. Walk forth in humility!

8/19/13 – In summary, it was just an ordinary day of work, somewhat mundane and pretty much business. I prayed a lot and sought wisdom because of feeling inadequate and also wanting to glorify and pursue God in everything. Sometimes, I was in tears as I closed my eyes and meditated on God, knowing that he is faithful and will give me what I need. I don't feel like I washed any feet, shared any love, or preached the name of Jesus. It was just a day, and I tried to live it for the Lord. I need to keep myself out of the way, keep my pride at bay, walk in humility and love, and lay everything down at the feet of Jesus. We'll see how tomorrow goes.

8/21/13 – I still feel flat and a lack of spiritual purpose. I really need help grasping the idea that I can serve the Lord with purpose no matter the "ministry" capacity. From a business perspective, I am highly productive. From a spiritual perspective, it all feels flat. The only thing I can do is continue taking things before the Lord on a regular basis and relying on him for wisdom and guidance— having a mind of continual prayer. As far as spiritual or shepherding influence, that is not happening yet. I presume it will take many months for that to start developing as the relationships tighten up. I need to continually feel that spiritual burden so it continues to drive me to the feet of Jesus. Hopefully that will soon translate into living like him.

8/5/14 (One year later) – It's been over a year since we got back from PNG and almost a year since I started working in business again. It's been a tough year at times, especially when I reflect back on our time in PNG. We miss it for sure, and we find ourselves struggling to find purpose in daily life sometimes. Yesterday, I had to read back through my journal entries from a year ago to remind myself how God was working in our lives. Sometimes, when we get jaded, we need to look back at those times of clarity and find encouragement.

To live out "church" in the business world—that was my original philosophy in coming back to Wildman. To truly make an impact on the lives of people, point them to Christ by way of my example, and challenge them to the believer's obligation of playing a part in God redeeming people from every tribe, tongue, and nation. Lord, help me to put my stake in the ground and live full of joy, peace, grace, and steadfastness in you.

No one said the journey would be easy. Jesus and the Apostles said it would cost us much, that we would face persecution, and that we would be sheep among wolves. It's a daily decision to lay aside our pride, our agenda, our selfishness, and look to God to direct our steps. Along the way, we are to be faithful and excellent in all we do, working for the Lord, not men.

We need work to meet much of our basic social, emotional, and psychological needs, and work needs us, too. It's what makes society go round. It's what gives us life, opportunity, and a future. It's a place where we spend the majority of our waking hours, and it's the place where we can be filled and pour into others.

But that is a choice. If we don't recognize the blessing of work, the alternative is to merely show up, collect a paycheck, have no mission, no purpose, and just drift through life, probably unsatisfied, unhappy, and unfulfilled.

God has so much more for us! Embrace his calling on your life to live missionally wherever you are and be a light to those around you. It will change your life and the lives of those around you.

Questions to Prayerfully Consider

- What if you believed your work was important and meaningful to God? How would that impact your day? How might that impact your fulfillment in life?

- What if you chose to focus on the presence of God throughout your day, in conversations, in your work, in your attitude? How might that impact your day and those around you?

- What if your co-workers and leadership team had a missional mindset? What if they worked with excellence as if working for the Lord? What kind of culture would that create?

- What might look different if tomorrow you chose to be a light to those around you? No matter how difficult, boring, or challenging the work is?

8

GOD IS THE OWNER

I came across a little book called *God Owns My Business* when I was in my mid-twenties, and it blew me away. In the book, I learned about a man named Stanley Tam, who started US Plastic Corp in 1936 with only $25 of his own money and a $12 loan from his dad. Soon after he started the business, however, he went broke.

Stanley was understandably discouraged. He went to the Lord in prayer, and he believed God told him that if he turned the business over to him, it would succeed. In response to that direction, Stanley gave 51 percent of the company's stock to a nonprofit organization, making God the majority owner.

Afterward, the business began to grow and perform well. Soon, Stanley was giving 60 percent of the profits to missions work and doing "exceedingly well" by keeping the other 40 percent.

In 1955, on a mission trip to South America, Stanley saw God work powerfully in people's lives. He gave a sermon through an interpreter, and he concluded his message by saying, "God is present here tonight. He speaks with deep conviction to many of your hearts. Let us bow our heads. If the Lord has spoken to your heart tonight, slip out of your pew and come to the altar here in front." As people began to come forward, Stanley felt frozen. The presence of God was powerful on him, and he began to reflect on the home he owned, the money in his bank accounts, his investments, and all of his success.

Stanley asked God what he wanted him to do, and he felt like God told him, "Stanley, I want you to become an employee of mine."

Stanley replied, "Isn't that what I am already doing?"

But God reminded him that they were business partners. Now, God wanted him to turn the entire business over to him!

It wasn't as easy as saying yes. Stanley wrestled with God and initially said he couldn't do it. He pleaded that 60 percent should be enough since most people don't even give God 10 percent! But God continued to reveal truth to Stanley through scripture, challenging him in his thoughts.

By the end of that trip, on January 15, 1955, Stanley made the commitment to God that he would no longer be a stockholder. All stock would belong to God. Since then, US Plastic Corp has cumulatively contributed more than $150 million to the work of God's Kingdom.

Living as Stewards

The Stanley Tam story seemed radical to me, but I shook it off because our generation that worked in the business did not own our family business at the time. But it did always stick with me in the back of my mind, that is until about 8 years later in 2014 when I read an article in TwoTen Magazine. There I read a story about another business owner who had built a business and then gave it away. At this point in my life, we had been back from the mission field for about a year, and earlier that year my brothers-in-law had given me an opportunity to become one of the owners. I was shaken again by another powerful story but this time it hit closer to home.

Alan and Katherine Barnhart met in college, got engaged, and once they got married had plans to move to a closed country under the umbrella of Alan's profession as a civil engineer so they could present the gospel in those hard-to-reach places.

They planned and trained to enter the mission field, but just before they were ready to launch, life threw them a curveball. Alan's parents had been running a family business and decided they were ready for a change and approached Alan about taking over the business. That business,

Barnhart Crane, was a small mom-and-pop company with about ten employees.

This created quite the predicament for Alan and Katherine as their hearts were already yearning for the mission field and they'd been preparing. For Katherine, in particular, it was her dream and her longing. Alan, however, began to feel led to take over the family business. They were at odds for a while, but after much discussion and debate, they finally agreed to run the business—though Katherine still felt conflicted.

Alan diligently studied the scriptures for a couple of years through the lens of running a business and he came with two primary conclusions. First: "the whole concept of ownership, that everything I have has come from God and belongs to God. My job is to be a steward and figure out what God wants me to do with his stuff." Second, he realized that business success could be detrimental to his life. He had seen what money and wealth had done to others, and he knew wealth is a tool the enemy can use to twist things and plant seeds of greed that grow and make a person self-serving and distracted from the purposes of God.

They made the decision early on to cap their lifestyle with a very modest salary so that, as the business grew, their lifestyle would stay the same. In doing so, they chose to break the connection between their income and their consumption and opened themselves up to accountability.

Barnhart started in 1969 with ten employees in one location and grew to over 1,000 employees in fifty locations. Through the hard work of a talented team, the company generated revenues from $1.5 million in 1986 to over $400 million in 2019. Alan states, "It was so far beyond our planning and our strategy; we just watched God do miracle after miracle and cause this company to be successful."

Alan and his brother chose to give away 50 percent of the profits and reinvest the other 50 percent into the continued growth of the business. The first year they had profit, they gave away $50,000. The next year, they gave $150,000. Eventually, as they continued to grow, they were able to give away $1 million in a single, successful year. In 2005, they were able to start giving away $1 million a month—a practice they have continued ever since.

The company was eventually worth hundreds of millions of dollars, and Alan and his brother discussed it and decided: "God owns this thing. Let's see if we can give it away." You see, they believed that God truly owned the business, and they were merely stewarding what God had entrusted to them. Today, National Christian Foundation owns 99 percent of the company, and the remaining 1 percent sits in a voting trust. God truly owns Barnhart, and he has done amazing things through the company to create Kingdom resources that help advance his causes. For further details on this story, check out barnhartcrane.com.

"What Must I Do?"

There are numerous stories just like Stanley's and Alan's, of men and women called into business to forsake the world and follow Jesus with wild abandon. They believe God owns their businesses, and they live like it. They view themselves as stewards of what God owns.

How did both Stanley and Alan arrive at such a radical conclusion? Because they were in a relationship with Jesus. They read the scriptures and had a heart for God's purpose to redeem a lost world. They spent time with God in conversation, communion, and prayer, and they responded when led by the Holy Spirit.

In Matthew 19:16-26, we read about Jesus having a conversation with someone who asks him, "What must I do to have eternal life?" As they discuss it, the man insists that he has kept all of the commandments and has faith in God. So then Jesus tells him, "If you want to be perfect, go and sell all your possessions and give the money to the poor, and you will have treasure in heaven. Then come, follow me."

After that, we're told "the man went away sad because he had many possessions."

Jesus then goes on to say, "It is very hard for a rich person to enter the Kingdom of Heaven," and it is "easier for a camel to go through the eye of a needle than for a rich person to enter the Kingdom of God." At this, it says that the "disciples were astounded." They couldn't believe what they had just heard. They thought this was an impossible demand that no one would be able to fulfill.

It then reads, "Jesus looked at them intently and said, 'With man this is impossible. But with God all things are possible'" (Matthew 19:26 NIV)[1].

On their own, pursuing business for themselves apart from a relationship with Jesus, Stanley and Alan might never have heard the Lord's voice speaking and leading them. If they did hear it, it probably would have been impossible for them to overcome their human desires and be obedient. However, because they did have a relationship with and had put their faith in Jesus, they were able to not only hear and be led by the Holy Spirit, but to walk in obedience to the Lord's leading. What would have been impossible for them on their own became possible with God.

After the second encounter with God, when he asked Stanley to turn over 100 percent of his business, Stanley went through an intense struggle. But God persevered and walked him through the impossibility. As a result, the next sixty-five years would be marked by incredible growth, impact, and millions of dollars generated towards missions. Not only were the results greater, but Stanley and his family's lives were greatly enriched. Once they "burned their ships" and surrendered completely to the Lord in obedience, their lives were forever changed, as were thousands of others around the world.

The acquisition of resources, wealth, and ownership appeals to most people, no matter how in love with Jesus they may be. For some, these things have a firm grip on their hearts. I, too, have wrestled with the desire for many years. I'm an entrepreneur, so I love generating resources to expand God's Kingdom. I believe in stewardship and that God is the owner of everything. I am merely entrusted to care for what he has given me. The questions I must continually grapple with are:

- How much do I keep of what belongs to God?
- What do I need?
- And how should I define "need" anyway?

My wife and I gave it all up in 2009 to follow God's call to move halfway around the world to the unfamiliar and distant country of Papua New Guinea. As we prepared to move from America to PNG, after all debts were settled with houses and cars, we had about $5,000 in the bank. We lived off support as missionaries for the next three and a half years.

When we later returned home to the US, we had seven suitcases for a family of six and a net worth of about $15,000 in a 401K. That was the sum total of our possessions, but we still managed to buy a house and slowly added necessary things like chairs, tables, and beds.

The mindset I had developed by the time we left Papua New Guinea was that our family could go anywhere and do anything because we had Jesus. He was all we needed, and I knew he would provide a roof over our heads and a way to feed my family. While we certainly faced many challenges, we also felt tremendous freedom and peace living completely dependent on God. What else did we need?

I had also developed the mindset of stewarding others' money. As missionaries, we lived off of donations and we felt a great responsibility to steward the resources well. People entrusted us to use the resources to meet our needs and support our ministry. When I re-entered the business world and started earning a paycheck I had to consider this idea of stewardship in the same way. God was providing the resources via my paycheck to meet my needs and support our ministry. Why is it so much harder to embrace this mindset when we are "earning" our income?

It's been ten years since we moved back and re-entered the business world. We've gone from seven suitcases to living modestly yet comfortably. Along the way, we have had to be intentional about not re-building ships and filling them with stuff. It's a constant effort to keep the ships deconstructed as our desires for comfort and ease slowly start rebuilding them.

But like Paul, we have "I know what it is to be in need, and I know what it is to have plenty." We've also "learned the secret of being content in any and every situation, whether well fed or hungry, whether living in plenty or in want."[2] I have experienced making a living for myself, and I also had a season of dependence on others.

After returning from Papua New Guinea, I was given the opportunity to become one of the owners of our family business. It has continued to grow rapidly, and today the value of the company is significant. So how will we steward? What is the true condition of my heart on this topic? Have I truly handed everything over to the Lord?

The Heart of the Matter

As I write this, I must confess it's a constant internal struggle, but I ask myself the tough questions—questions many people don't (or won't) ask. I want to serve God, and I want to invest all I have into the Kingdom, but I also want comfort. I want plenty of resources to travel, to serve, to give, to invest, to grow. I love those things. What is God asking of me?

If he asked me to give it all away, to sell all of my possessions and give the money to the poor, then come follow him, would I really do it? My wife and I did that once before when we moved to Papua New Guinea, so you might think it would be easy to do it again.

To be honest, there's a lot more at stake now. Company revenue is nearly seven times greater than it was before Papua New Guinea, and I feel energized at the thought of the company continuing to grow and do great things with the profits. But are we willing to give up control and totally surrender everything? When you own a company, you feel like you have control. It's hard to surrender *all* of it and relinquish control to God.

Like Stanley, we give away a good portion of our profits and reinvest most of the rest back into the company. Is God asking for some or all? And what does "all" look like? Years ago, just like Barnhart, we set a crazy goal of giving away $1 million a year. This year, we finally hit that goal. It's a great thing, but we still own this company. I still have my tiny grip on it because it belongs to us and we get to choose what we're going to do. So, the question remains: have I truly settled the ownership issue? Most importantly, have I fully committed my heart?

God's work through our company has been awesome. We are blessed with an incredible CEO who has a heart to use business as a vessel to impact lives. Under Josh's leadership over the last 12 years we have seen exponential growth and radical impact on people. I believe we have been faithful stewards, and God owns everything. But if God owns everything, does he really own our company? In other words, could we give up the ownership and control that enables us to use the resources for ourselves and families? What if God asked us to give it all up?

My initial response might be like Stanley's initial response: "But look, Lord, at how much of our profit we're giving away! Look at all the good stuff we're doing with missions. Can't we just keep doing that, living comfortably in abundance while also serving you and impacting lives?"

And, indeed, that may be what God would have us do. That may be what God wants *you* to do, too. But what if it isn't? What if he said, as he did to the young man in Matthew 19, "Go and sell everything and give it to the poor, then come and follow me." Would I do it? Would you?

That's what we really have to wrestle with. I pray often as David did in Psalm 139: 23-24 NIV: "Search me, God, and know my heart. Test me and know my anxious thoughts. See if there is any offensive way in me and lead me in the way everlasting."

A few years ago, we hired Bill High to help us sort through this struggle. Our family had been having conversations about what the future of the company should look like. What should it look like in 150 years? Should we continue to pass down ownership in the family? According to statistics, very few family businesses survive past the third generation. We've considered the same things Alan and Katherine Barnhart considered, that the money might lead to the destruction of family harmony and distract us from living the way Jesus would have us live.

How do we handle such a delicate topic? Our desire is to see our kids, grandkids, and the many generations to come thrive in life, in purpose, and in their relationship with Jesus. How might wealth or a transfer of wealth impact that?

Bill High focuses on helping families establish multi-generational legacies, with a particular emphasis on wealth stewardship. Our family has spent the last few years going through the process of what it looks like to put our company ownership in a trust that would then be governed by the family. We have several years of work ahead of us, but we are on the path and have a plan.

Eventually, we will have a family council that sits over the trust, with committees of family members that steward areas such as ministry investment (giving), family employment, family office investments, culture and education (teaching the next generation our Biblical family values), and reinvestment in the company. The ownership will sit in Delaware Dynasty Trust and God will, in effect, be the sole owner.

If you are a business owner, I encourage you to wrestle with these same thoughts and questions. Ask God what he would have you do. If he is the owner of everything, is he truly the owner? Join me on the same journey that pioneers such as Stanley and Alan have modeled for us.

Aside from the issues of stewardship vs. ownership, a company that is completely yielded to God and his purposes can make an enormous impact for the Great Commission with their resources. But there's more to it. When a company's leaders are fully yielded to God, there is a purpose for each and every employee that is greater than just a paycheck.

More than just directing resources externally, you can do a lot of great work internally with resources stewarded through the lens of Jesus. Not only can you create a generous culture with high engagement, inviting people into the giving and generosity, but you also have the opportunity to bring people into the purposes of God—to love them, to show them the light of Jesus, to create a culture that attracts employees to Jesus, to truly transform lives.

Once a company yields its resources completely to God, the company can become incredibly purposeful and generous in every way. The company becomes missional. It is fully about the work of God. After all, he owns it!

Questions to Prayerfully Consider

- What if you asked God if there is anything that he needs to own that you haven't let go of? What if you believed that God owned your business and you were just the chosen steward?

- What if you deeply considered what you're building and why? What type of legacy will you leave and what will you be remembered for?

- What if the gifts, abilities, intellect, and talent he gave you were not for your glory but his?

- What if you knew he had blessed you as an owner or business leader so that you could use what he has entrusted you to steward in order to be a blessing to others, to be a light on a hill that cannot be hidden?

- How would it change the way you lead, work, and treat your employees?

- How does this chapter impact your thoughts on stewardship and generosity?

9

WHAT IF LOVE WORKS?

He was a young man in his early twenties starting a new job. On the job, he soon made new friends and ultimately found Jesus. Through community and fellowship with his new friends and intentional discipleship from his boss, he ended up feeling called to the mission field, so he moved to the Dominican Republic to serve.

THEN THERE WAS a single mother of four struggling to make ends meet. She had little confidence and low self-esteem, and she had a hard time looking people in the eyes, as if she felt shame. However, she was hired by a boss who had compassion on her and saw beyond the lack of confidence. He believed she could be trained to do a good job in administrative and data entry work.

Her new co-workers helped bring her along, and her boss continued to affirm, coach, encourage, and train her. One day, she was given a devotional book by a coworker, which encouraged her in her faith journey, and she began attending church with her kids. She excelled on the job, and a newfound confidence emerged.

During her first Christmas season on the job, she didn't have much money for presents or a nice Christmas dinner; however, her boss intuitively picked up on this, and he invited her and her four kids to join his family on Christmas morning for breakfast and games.

Over the next few years, the single mother continued to grow in confidence, and her life really blossomed. Today, she is married, growing in her faith, confident, and in a great job.

~

THEY WERE POOR, a young couple struggling to make ends meet, with a mountain of debt. They lived in a dilapidated trailer, and at one point, they couldn't afford the gas bill so they had to huddle around the electric stove to get heat in the middle of winter. Still, they both managed to get new jobs—and at the same company.

On the job, they were introduced to several great programs, including Dave Ramsey's Financial Peace University which was offered by the company. They began applying Dave Ramsey's financial principles, including tithing, and were diligent in their efforts. They also began dreaming with the company's dream manager. They felt energized by the company culture and their coworkers, and they saw a real purpose in their work.

Over the next few years, they gradually paid off all of their debts and bought their first home. Their home became a wonderful place to raise their two kids. They both got promotions, and to this day, they are thriving in their work, their personal lives, and their spiritual lives. They have both become very generous and have an abundance mindset that says, "God always provides; we can't outgive God." They are influencers in their work community and play a big part in changing lives.

~

A MAN in his late sixties has prayed with hundreds of team members, sat at the bedside with the sick and dying, attended the funerals of loved ones, and been there when people needed him. He also discipled and dreamed with dozens of people on a regular basis. Several of those people changed the trajectory of their lives and chose the path of life in Jesus because of him. He serves as the company's corporate chaplain and dream manager.

HUNDREDS OF PEOPLE, including employees, family members, customers, and vendors, have gone on mission trips to the Dominican Republic to see the work being done by a ministry the company supports. Twice a year, they take employees and associates down there to witness firsthand the impact the company is making. The company has donated hundreds of thousands of dollars to this ministry, but beyond simply sending money, they are also working hard to ensure that their employees make the connection between the work they do and the impact they are having.

A CEO DROVE several hours to the streets of Indianapolis to rescue a struggling former employee who had gotten strung out on heroin and was on a path of destruction. The CEO found him on the streets and took him to a program called Teen Challenge. In the end, this saved the man's life and pointed him to Jesus, the ultimate healer, who set the man free from the bondage of addiction. Years later, this same man is now a regional director of Teen Challenge and travels around the country ministering, preaching, and sharing his story, motivating others to turn to Jesus.

A YOUNG MAN'S grandfather was on his deathbed, and he knew his grandfather didn't know Jesus. The company's corporate chaplain was summoned. He dropped everything and rushed to the hospital, where he presented the gospel. The dying man accepted Jesus as his savior. He soon passed away, but he is now rejoicing forever in heaven thanks to the work of the chaplain.

SHE WAS A QUIET, behind-the-scenes janitor who worked diligently to keep a facility clean, but she had some things in her own home that needed repaired and maintained. However, she lacked the means to pay for them.

A group of her team members at work became aware of her needs, so they organized a workday at her house. They sent her away for the day, and when she returned, she was amazed at how much work the team had done. She felt a deep sense of dignity and gratitude, which filled her life with light and encouragement.

EACH WEEK A GROUP of employees meets together to pray for those who are struggling, sick, or in need of any prayer. There is a prayer box where employees can submit requests, and each week the prayer group reads them and prays over the known and unknown requests of the company's employees and their families. Along the way, they've prayed some very specific prayers and seen incredible answers. It's a powerful behind-the-scenes ministry.

THE OWNERS of a company have been meeting every week for twenty years to pray over the company, decisions that need to be made, and any issues or struggles their employees or their families are facing. They have journaled the prayers and can look back and see God's faithfulness and the amazing power of prayer through it all.

EACH YEAR at their company Christmas party, they bring in a well-known guest speaker or artist, including people like Jeremy Camp, Michael Jr., Bob Goff, Big Daddy Weave, and Jase Robertson, to name a few. Each artist or speaker offers an entertaining message but, most importantly, it's an intentional message about Jesus. It's an opportunity for the company to connect with their nearly 500 employees and guests through a Christmas party that is designed to be fun, engaging, and powerfully challenging.

Many have made decisions to follow Jesus during these Christmas celebrations.

~

AN EMPLOYEE WAS STRUGGLING with addiction, which led to him losing his job. His boss gathered up a few friends and went to his house one night to meet with him and his wife. They urged him to get help and took him to a recovery center, where he stayed for a year. He has been sober for years, is an engaged father and husband, has a great job, and, most importantly, is following Jesus.

Ministry First, Business Second

Cars have been repaired, houses fixed up, bills paid when there was no hope. Thousands of dollars have been reinvested into helping dozens of employees, customers, and others in the community in times of need. People have had help with adoptions, missions trips, and just about any major expense where there was a financial need that's hard to meet in certain seasons of life.

From practical goals to lifetime dreams—goals have been accomplished through the dream management program. First time homes have been purchased, debts have been paid down, relationships have been restored, college degrees have been completed, and lives have been spiritually changed. People are growing financially, physically, intellectually, and most importantly in their faith. Some have discovered life in Jesus, others are on the journey and being challenged to grow deeper.

Dozens of married couples have had their marriages rejuvenated and refreshed during marriage retreats. The only cost they need to cover is the airfare, the rest is handled by the company. They are spiritually fed with principles about living out marriage as a mission. For many, these retreats have changed the trajectory of their marriage and their families.

Millions of dollars have been given away to nonprofits in the community and around the world. Churches have been planted, wells have been dug, jobs have been created, and hope and light are shining in dark places. Thousands of additional paid time-off days have been utilized for acts of service since employees can use up to five additional PTO days each year to serve locally or abroad.

When a team member is struggling with a medical issue in their family, co-workers rally around them and put together meal trains, pitch in money to cover travel expenses to and from a hospital or medical center, and provide gifts of comfort. There is a culture of having each other's backs when things get tough.

I could fill an entire book with stories like these. When reading through them, you might think they came out of a church. And, in fact, they did. But this church happens to be a business. It's a business that is a ministry first and a business second. What is the name of this company? Wildman Business Group, which I have been part of helping lead and steward with my family for over two decades.

We believe we are just beginning to see what God can really do through leaders and a company that are yielded to the purposes of God. We are still learning, still dreaming, and still asking ourselves how we can reflect Jesus better. In everything, we desire to lead missionally, transform the lives of our employees, and produce purposeful profit that can be given away to impact our community and our world for the sake of the gospel.

The stories I've shared are just a few examples of how love works and how it can transform lives, even in the workplace. This is important because, after all, most people spend a majority of their time at work. The average full-time worker will spend 70,000 to 80,000 hours at work over the course of their lifetime. That's more hours spent at work than pretty much any other activity in life.

Clearly, then, there is no better opportunity for ministry than at work. There is no better opportunity to live out the love of God and extend it to others.

Leaders, we have an opportunity to shape culture and change the world! We have an opportunity to live as ambassadors and create an environment that draws people to Jesus!

A lot of the most impactful work happens in the small acts, the unexpected conversations, and most importantly through consistency of character and trust. Truett Cathy, the founder of Chick-fil-A, was quoted as saying, "You don't have to make headlines to make a difference." This is so true. It's in the small things. It starts with simple things like a smile, a kind word, asking about life and doing so with authenticity.

People think they must have some special gift to make a difference, or that they don't have enough Bible knowledge to make a difference. Let me assure you: you have the power to make someone's day better! It's not that complicated.

I learned this lesson from my dear mother, Rose. She is the sweetest and most positive person on the planet. Wherever she goes and whoever she is talking to, she brings hope and cheer. This rubbed off on me over the years, and I think I was also blessed with those positive genes (thanks, mom!). When I was a kid, she used to tell me, "You can catch more bees with honey than you can vinegar." This old-time saying has stuck with me for years.

So, do you have the power to make someone's day better? Yes, it's simple. Just be honey (sweet) to those around you and not vinegar (sour)!

This is how the seeds are planted, how relationships are forged, and how trust is built. It's how character is demonstrated over time. This is the foundation. Everyone who is a follower of Jesus has been given the ability to be a light to a dark world. As we each grow in our relationship with God, we become empowered in new and different ways to continue spreading the light.

As great as the outcomes may sound, and as simple as they might be, there are also plenty of difficulties on this journey. As owners and leaders, we sometimes get black eyes or stub our toes. We are merely humans trying to be led by the Holy Spirit, resist our sin nature, and do what's right, stewarding our company, resources, and people according to the will of God. Human sin and the corruption of the world work against us to confuse the order, to create chaos, and to make relationships difficult.

Even as we pursue true wisdom from the Bible and seek Godly discernment, we can still end up going down the wrong path. Graeme Goldsworthy says it well in his book *According to Plan*, "This means that human sinfulness not only upsets relationships but also renders us, even as believers, prone to misunderstanding and false thinking."[1]

Thankfully, we are under grace and the regenerating power of God, who is in the business of redeeming people, of taking our brokenness and making it something wonderful. When we embrace God's work of redemption, it helps us view the people we lead and the work we do through a different lens. It empowers us to steward an organization that is playing a part in God's story of being a light in this dark world.

Yes, we can play a role in his redemptive plan in the context he's placed us in, even the workplace! As business leaders, we can bring hope and inspiration, acting as ambassadors of Christ entrusted with the ministry of reconciliation to see broken and hurting souls redeemed and reconciled to God through Jesus Christ.

According to ComPsych,[2] 62 percent of US workers have high levels of stress with extreme fatigue, 33 percent have constant but manageable stress, and only 5 percent have low stress levels. Another study by Zippia Research[3] shows that 76 percent of US workers report that workplace stress affects their personal relationships, and more than 50 percent of workers are not engaged at work as a result of stress.

According to National Alliance,[4] 83 percent of US workers are currently experiencing mental health problems, and 40 percent don't believe their employer cares about their mental health beyond simply being productive at their job.

Wake Up and Lead

Jesus-following leaders, let's wake up! "This is why it is said, 'Wake up, O sleeper, rise from the dead, and Christ will shine on you.' Be very careful then how you live—not as unwise, but as wise, making the most of every opportunity, because the days are evil. Therefore, do not be foolish, but understand what the Lord's will is" (Ephesians 5:14-17 NIV)[5].

Understand what the Lord's will is. In scripture, his will is clearly revealed for all matters of life—yes, even business. Even how to be excellent in your work, how to care for people, how to live a Godly life, how to spread the gospel, how to deal with conflict, and how to grow in faith and righteousness. It's all in there!

Since this chapter is specifically about how love as an action can play out in the workplace, let's look at two verses that highlight a key responsibility for leaders. If you are a follower of Jesus and in a position of leadership, you have been given the responsibility to steward the assets, people, and profits toward the purposes of God. Proverbs 3:27 says, "Do not with-

hold good from those to whom it is due when it is in your power to act."[6]
As a leader, you have been empowered to act. In Romans 13:4-5, Paul says,
"For the one in authority is God's servant for your good."[7]

So what if you viewed your employees as people? Broken, hurting
people who are redeemed by God's incredible grace? Everyone has something going on in their lives, and difficult seasons come and go. As leaders,
we need to be mindful of this and intentionally create a culture of grace.
We, too, have garbage in our lives, and if we act like we don't, everyone
around us will sense at some point that we are phony.

Let's embrace the fact that we are all sinners saved by grace, and we
are all trying to work out our salvation and grow. Let's develop a sense of
compassion, grace, and empathy for each other. This will create true
harmony, true fellowship, and a workplace where God can do amazing
things in our lives.

Realize that every employee, co-worker, and teammate is just like you.
We have bills, problems, struggles, strained relationships, and worries.
You might not be able to solve their problems, help them raise their children, or get them out of debt, but you can come alongside them and make
their jobs more rewarding, creating an environment of openness, trust,
and growth.

What does this look like practically-speaking? Again, it's not complicated. As a leader, simply reflect on how much time you spend getting to
know your employee. Have conversations with them. Ask them what is
important to them. What makes them tick? What inspires them and gives
them hope? How are they feeling today? How about their work? Are the
expectations of their job clear? Put yourself in their shoes, in their jobs.
What would make it more fun, rewarding, and engaging? Through these
conversations trust is built, the employee discovers that you care for them,
and you maintain an open door to positively influence their lives and be
the light of Christ to them.

What if you cultivated a love for every employee that stemmed from
your love of Jesus? I am referring to agape love, which means "to will to
the good of another, to be deliberate, a love that is the result of choices
and behaviors rather than feelings and emotions."

This kind of love is action-oriented and based on a determination to
love as an act regardless of the person or their performance. Whether an

employee is performing well or poorly, love can (and should) still be shown. I have had to walk through dozens of terminations over the years, and some were good friends. Even then, I tried to demonstrate love in how I handled the situation.

Leaders assume you can't create this kind of culture, this kind of love, this kind of environment that draws people to Christ, and at the same time maintain a culture of excellence and accountability. This couldn't be further from the truth, and it's not Biblical.

Start by Dreaming

Twenty years ago, my brother-in-law Josh Wildman and I attended the Global Leadership Summit in Chicago. It was the first time we were challenged about the idea of "faith in the marketplace." A lightbulb went off for us, and we were ignited!

On the return trip back, Josh drove while I worked on my laptop, typing out "God's Plan For Wildman." This document had some far-fetched dreams of what could be possible someday, ideas like giving away $1 million a year, coordinating marriage retreats in Hawaii, taking team members on mission trips and giving extra paid vacation days to do so, prayer gatherings, Bible studies, above market wages, and so many more dreams.

The crazy thing is, nearly all of these far-fetched dreams have been accomplished (or are in the process of being accomplished) and then some! But it started with dreaming about what was possible in an organization whose purpose is to serve God and make him known—to do business as a ministry, putting God first and people a close second.

Start by dreaming. It doesn't matter how crazy the ideas seem, write them down and dream. Little by little over time you will be amazed at what God will do. Start simple and trust God to show you how to lead your organization or your team.

- What if you lived and believed that Jesus could use you to make a difference?
- What if God wanted to use you to create a culture of sacrificial community, fellowship, and support?

- What if you focused on helping your employees discover their God-wired purpose in life and empowered them to do something about it?
- What if your business was a gathering place for prayer, or even worship?
- What if you could be a part of a revival in the marketplace?
- What if you could create a company culture that was life-giving and a place of hope and inspiration?
- What if co-workers were considered family—for some, it may be the closest to family they ever experience.

Maybe this all sounds a bit "churchy" to you. You might be thinking, "We are a business, after all, and we have work to do!" I would argue—and I can prove from our own experiences—all of this can certainly be done, even while driving value, working with excellence, and maintaining a culture of high accountability.

In fact, a purposeful culture can make your employees even more engaged, leading to a business that is better, more productive, and more profitable. This kind of workplace is life-giving and fulfilling. Look, most people want to do excellent work. When they feel cared for, invested into, and have clarity of expectations, they will perform well, stay engaged, and have lower turnover.

If we are going to spend 80,000 hours working together, we ought to do everything we can to make it life-giving, purposeful, fulfilling, and transformative. Love works. This is the essence of missional leadership.

My friends, "Let us not love with words or speech but with actions and in truth" (1 John 3:18 NIV)[8].

I would like to wrap up this chapter with what I believe is the most important message for leaders in this book. It is clear in scripture that we are to make disciples of all nations. It is clear that we are to keep our neighbor, our community, our state, our region, our country, and our world in full view. We have a responsibility as leaders to make disciples of those within our sphere of influence. Our sphere of influence may be localized, but the vision is global.

Imagine if, during your career, you raised dozens of disciples, some of whom even went into full-time overseas missions, carrying the gospel to the least reached places of the world.

Leaders, if we are followers of Jesus, we must lead with the Great Commission in full view. It must become the lens we see everything through. Ultimately, that is the purpose! God has entrusted you to care for his flock. This includes being his ambassador and representing his light so he can work within the people you have influenced to raise up more disciples for his cause.

Questions to Prayerfully Consider

- What if love really works? What does scripture say about love? If you believe love works, what ideas do you have for embracing this philosophy in the way you lead your team and organization?

- What are some steps you could take to be more intentional with your culture and how people are treated, cared for, and empowered?

- What would it look like to more intentionally show through your actions the love of Jesus to your employees or teammates?

- List the dreams you have for your company about what's possible. What do you believe God could do through you or your company that he hasn't done yet? What kind of impact do you dream of?

10

THE MOST IMPORTANT RESULTS

By most standards, Stephen L. Bryant should have been dead long ago—at best, he should have remained a poor Kentucky hillbilly. He tasted death at least nine times. He's beaten the Jumanji record of three lives, and although I'm pretty sure he's not a cat, he has cracked the cat kingdom's code of defying mortality.

Growing up in poverty was difficult, but as a young boy, Steve didn't know any better. He thought having one restroom—an outhouse—and eating groundhogs for dinner was normal. And, in fact, he *was* a normal boy, but he lived in very abnormal circumstances, circumstances that were highly unlikely to provide any chance for a better life. Even so, at ten years old, he already knew he wanted to escape poverty and do something significant with his life. An inner ember of motivation burned brightly, a spark that he would later fan into a flame of courage and a relentless determination for success.

Steve was rambunctious and a prankster, often finding himself getting in trouble or into fights. Actually, he liked a good fight, so he often picked them.

Picture a fourteen-year-old boy with his hair slicked back by grease from the previous night's groundhog dinner, cut-off jean shorts, a flannel shirt with the sleeves cut short then rolled up to his shoulders with a pack of smokes nestled inside. One cig was often dangling from his mouth, an extra one tucked behind his ear, just in case. He sometimes had a bottle of moonshine in his back pocket. Sort of a rougher, more redneck version of the boys from *The Dukes of Hazzard*.

At the age of nineteen, Steve joined the United States Marine Corps, where he put his restlessness to work. He soon found himself in the middle of the Vietnam War, enduring brutal combat and countless physical and mental challenges. Although he avoided any life-altering physical wounds, the psychological wounds he obtained were profoundly painful. He became a decorated veteran and was honorably discharged after the war.

Thank you, Steve, for your courageous service!

Steve re-entered society and went back to what he knew before the Marine Corps, working to survive. His work ethic was unmatched, and he had determination and an uncanny wit (with a sassy, colorful mouth!). Steve has a knack for figuring things out quickly, and he out-works everyone around him. In short order, he became incredibly successful as the youngest superstore manager in America for The Kroger Company.

Soon after, he had an opportunity to get into the commercial laundry business as a sales manager. He accepted the position and pursued it with the same sense of relentlessness, pouring over industry articles, trade publications, and asking questions of every kind. As a result, he became a sales expert and quickly moved up the ranks. From there, new, high-level opportunities arose, and over the next fifty years, he filled senior-level and executive-level roles in numerous laundries, ultimately becoming CEO and COO of three $150-million-plus public companies.

Eventually, he and his wife, Pam, decided to use their laundry expertise to start a consulting business, Concept XI Consulting. They figured they could make a lot more money, work a lot less, and help independent laundries conquer the industry along the way.

This is where Steve's story intersects with our story. Through industry relationships, Brent Wildman, the owner of Wildman Business Group at the time, crossed paths with Steve Bryant. Brent believed God would use Steve to help double the size of his company and train the next generation to take over and keep it going. In the year 2000, Steve became CEO of Wildman. Not only did he double the size of the company, he did it three times over twelve years and trained all of us along the way.

Reflecting on those years with Steve, I believe there was a reason God spared Steve's life so many times. God was preparing him for this professional assignment, knowing it would be the catalyst for a trajectory of growth and purpose for Wildman. It would also be the place where Steve's faith and work would come together for the first time. The old rough, tough, and gruff worldly heathen would finally become an integral part of a purpose-driven business that would change lives, generate purposeful profit, and create eternal impact for generations.

Steve and Pam were experts in their field. I learned so much from both of them, especially as an early-twenties know-it-all. They provided a good balance of encouragement and humility as they would occasionally call me out when my big head didn't fit through the door.

Steve wasn't bashful with his thoughts, no matter how derogatory they sounded. He said what he thought, didn't sugar coat anything, and included colorful adjectives and interesting name-calling. At fifty years old, he had only recently put his faith in Jesus and was figuring out what that meant for him.

In his growing faith, Steve was disciplined about studying the scriptures, and he genuinely cared for people. He would regularly drill me on scripture trivia and ask thought-provoking questions about various doctrines or Biblical stories. Regarding people, both Steve and Pam would go out of their way to lend a helping hand to the less fortunate, the struggling, and any who needed rescuing—and most of the time, those were employees. While he may have been tough, he demonstrated a deep care for every employee's well-being, and I know he loved us and always had our back.

Steve was a business genius, and part of his genius was keeping things simple and refusing to tolerate anything stupid—"stupid" being defined as overcomplicating things, confusing things, or drifting from the tried-and-true fundamentals. He drove clarity, accountability, and simplicity, and he knew how to get results.

Steve's most frequently used saying was, "What gets measured, gets managed." He knew that anything we measured against a goal would have a significantly greater chance of being accomplished, and he embedded this into our fabric. It became vital in getting us to where we are today.

Biblical Measuring

From a Biblical perspective, we see the practice of measuring all throughout scripture. In the beginning, God created the heavens and the earth, with implied measurements such as how long it took and the numbers of various things, and he defined the result as good. He gave very specific measurements to Noah for the Ark. He told Abraham how long Israel would be captive in Egypt. He provided Moses with specific measurements on collecting manna (about three quarts per person with no leftovers permitted), and he also gave Moses measurements for the tabernacle.

In John chapter 2, at the wedding in Cana, John records the number and size of the jars used for wine. Later in the chapter, at the feeding of the 5,000, the Apostles measure five loaves and two fish, which Jesus then multiplies miraculously to feed the crowd. Afterward, the leftovers are measured.

Jesus also measured the faith of various people. He uses terms like *lack of faith* (Matthew 6:30, 8:26, 14:31,16:8), *great faith* (Matthew 15:28), *according to your faith* (Matthew 9:29). Love is described and measured in various ways throughout the New Testament by Jesus and the Apostles.

And regarding the culmination of his plan of redemption, God established objectives, goals, and expected outcomes:

Objective (Jesus' mission): "Go therefore and make disciples of all nations" (Matthew 28:19 NIV)[1].

Lead Measurement/Goal (human activity/role): "And this gospel of the Kingdom will be preached in the whole world as a testimony to all nations, and then the end will come" (Matthew 24:14 NIV)[2].

Lag Measurement/Outcome (the work of God in the hearts of people): "After this I looked, and behold, a great multitude that no one could number, from every nation, tribe, people, and language standing before the throne and before the Lamb" (Revelation 7:9 ESV)[3].

I could go deep on this subject, but for now, I simply want to provide enough reference to establish the Biblical basis for setting goals and measuring things. I encourage you to study the topic deeper.

When it comes to business and making a Kingdom impact, what should we measure? How do we move beyond simply talking about the outcomes we would like to make? How do we move from *wishing* our culture could be different to actually *making* it different? If we are operating as ambassadors of Christ and stewards of His assets, people, and resources for the sake of expanding God's Kingdom, what should progress look like? If "what gets measured, gets managed" is a critical component to meeting goals and desired results, what should our approach as missional leaders be?

We need to be faithful to what God's word says. We need to trust the Holy Spirit to guide us to play our part in discipling the nations, whether that's preparing the soil, planting the seed, or watering, while trusting that God is going to make it grow.

Does that mean God is responsible for the outcome? Yes, I think that's exactly what it means. Jesus is the center of the story, and all we do should reflect him and his work.

We are called to be obedient in whatever role he calls us to play in his plan of redemption, while he works out his plans and purposes. Jesus will produce the desired outcome, which he has already set actions, timetables, and goals for.

Another one of my mentors, Steve Longbrake, always challenged the board, our CEO, and our executive leadership team with these questions: What are the spiritual inputs that will lead to life change? What are the lead activities we can do to create the best opportunity for heart transformation?

We can strategize, plan, and measure the inputs, but the outcome, God's work of heart transformation, is a mystery only known to God, and in some ways, it's practically impossible to measure. What we can measure are the inputs and activities that are lead indicators impacting the desired outcome.

Indeed, while difficult, there are some ways we can qualitatively measure the outcome of heart transformation, such as new fruit being displayed in various ways because of the transformational journey. Through our chaplaincy program, for example, we also measure the verbal commitments of people putting their faith in Jesus.

While these types of outcomes can be measured to some degree, it's not the same as measuring objective and controllable metrics such as revenue, sales, production efficiency, and customer satisfaction. Ultimately, as mere humans, we cannot know the true condition of another person's heart for certain, including if they have fully placed their faith in Jesus as Lord and Savior. Therefore, we just need to be obedient to the work God has called us to and trust him to make faith grow.

If your purpose (and your organization's purpose) is to be missional for the sake of the gospel, then what should the results look like? If your P&L is amazing, but you're failing to lead your people, invest in them, disciple them, show them the love of Christ, and accomplish the mission, should you still get a performance bonus given your purpose and vision? Should you get a pat on the back and a "job well done," maybe even a raise?

If our performance metrics are purely financially driven, then we can expect that we will get primarily financial results. Even the most committed Christians will perform how they are incentivized to perform, so we must consider what results we are rewarding and look for ways to keep a healthy balance in order to make sure our primary purpose is being accomplished.

Of course, all companies need to be financially sound, profitable, and growing, for where there is no profit margin there is no mission. Profit is the lifeblood of any business, something we need to live!

But what if your profits come at the expense of your primary purpose? What if Kingdom work is underperforming but your finances are overperforming? How will you adjust? Are you comfortable with excellent P&L results if your real purpose is compromised or ineffective? Are you willing to adjust profitability, if that's what it takes, to make sure you are relentlessly pursuing the purpose? After all, Jesus asks us to follow him wherever, however, and whatever the cost. If it is costly to follow Jesus and make him known, what does that look like for us and for our businesses?

Even if you are pursuing purposeful profit, you must still be careful that you don't overpursue this noble endeavor and create unhealthy families and lives along the way. It's a common practice even for Christian business leaders to reward only on financial metrics and P&L results, even if that means strained marriages, unhappy people, and stress. Are you encouraging harder work, working more, whatever it takes to accomplish financial goals? Are you thinking about rallying the troops for another aggressive growth budget? To what end?

As business leaders, we need to challenge ourselves to think differently.

Prioritize Your Focus

What if our most important priority was not the bottom line? What could it look like? What *should* it look like?

Brandon Schafer, founder of Five Capitals, which is where I received my coaching certification, addressed these questions by creating a framework called The Prioritized Leader. It goes like this:

At Five Capitals, we coach leaders on the importance of prioritizing their focus in this order:

- **Purpose** – Knowing and living the why of your organization.
- **People** – Investing, empowering, encouraging, discipling, and holding accountable.
- **Pace** – Discerning how fast or slow the organization should move to sustain long-term success and health while capitalizing on opportunities.
- **Perception** – Choosing a growth mindset and being open to creative solutions and new ideas.
- **Profit** – The effective management, stewardship, and release of an organization's resources.

The idea is that if these priorities get out of order or imbalanced, it will create unhealthy areas that could compromise your purpose.

Knowing your **purpose** and having a plan to accomplish that purpose is the first step. Knowing your **people** and having a plan to develop them, disciple them, and help them accomplish their dreams is the next priority. Keeping a healthy work environment and **pace** will provide the proactive growth mindset (**perception**) to be learning, growing, adapting, and innovating. And lastly, when all of these things are functioning effectively, the chances of **profitability** are significantly greater.

A simple way to boil this down is "seek first his Kingdom and righteousness, and all these things will be given to you" (Matthew 6:33 ESV)[4]. When we seek God and the purpose he has for us first, and we work diligently with excellence to honor God, he will provide the fruit that is needed to sustain us.

Here's the irony most Christians face in America. People look back on their lives and feel proud that they've dedicated so much to their careers. Great salary, good bonuses, and a lot of material possessions that they worked hard to obtain. They made many sacrifices on the altar of success. But their spouse and kids don't share their enthusiasm for their devotion to their career. They don't necessarily feel thankful that their spouse or parent was not the spiritual leader they could have been because their job sucked so much capacity out of them. All the family got were a few scraps of time at the end of each day. They would gladly have taken less income and fewer material possessions for more quality time.

That hard worker drove the train relentlessly and accomplished impressive financial goals. Hip hooray! All of those hours, blood, sweat, and tears, as well as compromised relationships with family and God.

That's what a lot of business leaders do, and it's how they incentivize their employees to act. Bonuses and pay raises encourage overworking at the expense of more meaningful things. Spouses, kids, and countless others pay the price.

As a business leader, you have the power to influence and shape a culture that will contribute to either creating healthy families or destroying them. I think God's will about this is crystal clear.

If we want to be faithful and diligent in the work God has called us to, we must stay focused on his purpose, while at the same time building a sustainable, profitable business. We need to set goals and measure performance to those goals not only for traditional performance metrics, but also our spiritual and cultural inputs and activities that will lead to transformed lives.

A missional leader focuses on expanding the gospel while at the same time stewarding the business they lead with excellence. I will tell you from experience, this journey is fulfilling and rewarding. Our company has experienced the beauty of it, and I believe this can happen for you in your business, too.

Questions to Prayerfully Consider

- What if God had an amazing culture in mind for your business? What is your dream for your culture? What does it look like?

- What lead measurements and inputs could you focus on to be more intentional about creating the God-centered culture you are dreaming of?

- What would the lag indicators be? What might success look like for these dreams? How might God define what that success looks like?

- How do you feel about the possibility that incentivizing employees to hit financial results has damaged their spiritual or family health? What guardrails could you put in place to ensure that personal and family health isn't compromised to achieve company objectives?

- In what order do you feel you have prioritized the following? Purpose, People, Pace, Perception, and Profit.

PART III

THE REST OF THE STORY

11

THE HARD STUFF

In 2007, I received a call from a friend in Nashville who said that Hunter Smith, the Indianapolis Colts punter, was looking for a guitarist for his Christian band. I thought it sounded like a cool opportunity, and the band was based out of Indianapolis, which wasn't too far to occasionally attend band practice. It had been about six years since Bobbi and I had moved back to Warsaw, Indiana after living in Nashville.

I'd studied music at Belmont University but dropped out when I had the chance to tour around the country, playing in everything from small venues to some of the largest sports arenas in front of thousands. I loved music and dreamed of playing guitar as a profession, but after living on a tour bus and traveling all over the place, I realized my greater dream of being married and creating a family was not wholly compatible with being on the road. After Bobbi and I married in 2000, I settled for studio session work in Nashville, and then ultimately, we moved home in August of 2001 to help with the family business.

When I got the call to play with Hunter, it set flame to the musical ember within. I was already well established in the family business and had no intention of leaving, but I thought exploring this as a side gig might be kind of cool. After praying about it, I decided to accept the gig, with no intention other than exploring the opportunity and engaging my musical gift once again.

After about six months in the band, God brought me to my knees. I felt strongly that he was asking me to leave the family business, give up future ownership in the company, and pursue music full-time.

I remember that decision point vividly. I then approached the band and told them, "I'm all in." However, I did not tell anyone else other than my wife. Bobbi and I struggled with the decision. I was giving up future ownership and security in the family business, but that meant we might also have to give up the dream home we'd worked so hard to build.

The amount of internal struggle surprised us. Why was it so hard to give up material things to follow God's will? We were disappointed at how the world had a grip on us, even after our experience in Honduras. We looked to God's word and realized that following him might cost us our worldly desires and comforts. Scripture is very clear about this. Some of the more difficult verses of the Bible had become a reality for us.

We lingered in a state of severe tension for about two weeks, until God spoke to me again. This time, he clearly said, "Now that I know where your heart is, I want you to stay where you are."

I suppose God knew there was only one thing that could divert my attention from the prospect of being one of the owners of the family business and an opportunity to build wealth. Only music could pull me away. Only music could get me to a point where I would say, "Yes, I will follow and say no to my worldly desires." So, he brought me to that decision point to see what I would do. It was simply a test of my heart.

Through that process, God once again released our grip on the world, and our hands began to open. After the perspective shift in Honduras in 2006, this test of surrender in 2007 made us truly willing to follow him wherever he led us.

Within less than a year, we were challenged once again to give up and surrender. In 2008, Bobbi and I read the book *Crazy Love* by Francis Chan, and it impacted us deeply. The two biggest convictions were the chapter "Profile of the Lukewarm" and the radical testimonies of people who gave up their worldly pursuits to follow God in wholehearted devotion.

We read the stories of people who gave up their jobs and moved to third world countries, people who gave away their possessions or downsized their homes to give more, and it all seemed so crazy! But it triggered a memory of the corporate executive we'd met on our first trip to

Honduras, a man who had given up his lucrative executive position to serve the poor, and the feelings I experienced on that trip came back with overwhelming conviction.

God used this study and reflection to stir our spirit once again. During this time we felt God asking us to sell our dream home and downsize for no other reason than out of sheer obedience to Him. The thought of giving up the home that "I" had designed and built was gut-wrenching, but we felt we had no choice except to follow God.

Stay or Go

We went through the process of getting the house ready to sell and listing it. The night of our first showing, Bobbi and I both felt peace and contentment. And again, God gently nudged me, "Now that I know where your heart is, I want you to stay right where you are."

Once again, he wanted to see that we would wholeheartedly give up our worldly goods for his sake. We reflected on the story of Abraham offering his son Isaac as a sacrifice. At the moment when Abraham was finally about to take action on God's request, God intervened and stopped him. He told Abraham it was just a test to see if his heart was fully committed.

Now, Bobbi and I had been tested in a similar way twice within a single year. God made a request of us, we showed our willingness to follow through, but then he intervened and kept us where we were. We began to suspect that God was doing this to prepare us for something big, but we didn't yet know what it was.

In the winter of 2008, we started going through a study called *Experiencing God*. During the study, God began to stir something within us even more. We knew something major was coming, but we still didn't know what it would be. I thought maybe he was going to ask me to start preaching more at work.

I'd been leading Bible studies at work for a few years, and was working with my three brother-in-laws to bring "God's Plan for Wildman" to life in an attempt to bring Christ into the workplace to drive life change through the business. I thought he might ask me to do more of that, even if it required taking a different position in the company. The most radical move in my mind would have been God asking me to leave the business to go work at our local church.

Finally, on March 2, 2009, God spoke. I heard him clearly, with fear and trembling. I wrote down what he said to me in my journal that morning: "It's time to dedicate your life to spreading the good news of Christ."

That was it. That's what God said to me. But what did it mean? I knew it must mean something far different from what I was currently doing, but God did not provide me with a clear picture of what it would look like.

I asked my wife to seek the Lord in her quiet time that morning, and then I left for the office. I stopped by the house later that day to see if she'd heard anything from him but when I went inside, I found her a complete mess. She had been crying, and she was emotionally distraught.

She looked at me and said, "Did God tell you we're supposed to move to Papua New Guinea?"

"Well, no, not exactly," I replied, "but based on what he said this morning, it makes sense."

And at that moment, our lives changed radically. A new course of action had been set before us.

We began a process of earnestly praying, seeking direction and affirmation, and waiting on God to show us each step of the way ahead. We sometimes wondered if we were going crazy. What if we'd heard wrong? What if this was some impulsive spiritual hero decision that was not actually God's will for us?

As we processed this new calling and reflected on how God had been working the previous few years, our faith grew and we kept choosing to trust the process. God had prepared us by opening our eyes in Honduras, by testing us to give up our business, wealth, and dream home. In doing so, he brought us to a place where we could hear and accept this call to go. Our hearts had been made ready.

After about six weeks of praying and seeking confirmation, we decided to tell my wife's parents. I was afraid of disrupting the successorship plan of the business. I was also nervous about taking Brent's daughter and grandchildren to some far flung island in the South Pacific with an uncertain return. Oddly enough, my in-laws had just returned a few weeks earlier from visiting a missionary family in the deep jungle of Papua New Guinea, a place none of us had ever visited before.

With questionable courage, I shared with them how God had been working in us over the previous few years. I told them we believed God was calling us to sell everything and move to Papua New Guinea.

Brent took a deep breath and burst into tears, and I thought, "Oh, man, what have I done?" After a moment of not being able to talk, he finally collected himself and told us he'd made a commitment to God as they left Papua New Guinea while looking back at the island through the airplane window:

"I will give whatever you ask of me to further your gospel in this country."

At that time, he thought he was yielding his finances. Little did he know that it would not only be finances but giving up his children and grandchildren! This was one of the greatest points of confirmation for us.

We then broke the news to my parents. My mom was thrilled that we were following God, but she was scared for our family. We were taking away her only grandchildren, which made it gut-wrenching. I processed this emotion through a song I wrote for her called "Three Little Angels." We had three kids at the time and they were my mom's pride and joy.

The Lord shared with me some words of encouragement for her that became the chorus to the song:

You will dance for eternity with them.

The pain and the sorrows will be wiped away forever.

The tears that you cry longing to hold them will turn into songs as you dance with them forever.

We had to have an eternal perspective. We didn't know when we would return, and we didn't know how long God would keep us there. It was incredibly difficult to leave our family with an unknown return.

We continued telling other family members and then team members in the business. Every conversation was difficult, there were lots of questions, and we just had to persevere and trust that we'd heard God clearly and correctly.

So, we listed our house in October of 2009, and we moved out in

December. I fully expected that because we were following God he would just take care of the house. I had heard stories of people knocking on the front door and offering cash, and since we were making a big sacrifice for God, I imagined that something amazing like that would happen to us, too. That did not prove to be the case, and it was a hard lesson in humility for me.

In January 2010, I worked my last day in the business, as we prepared to leave in February. By God's design, my work permit got held up and we were unable to leave the country until July. We had no vehicle, most of our possessions were sold or given away, and we'd moved out of our house to put it on the market. We were living with Brent and Karen, I had no job, and our suitcases were packed and ready to go.

We had burned our ships. There was no going back. Now, it was just a waiting game.

Every morning for six months, I woke up expecting to see an email from the Papua New Guinea government telling me my visa was ready so we could book our airfare. Every day for six months, I woke up expecting we were two weeks away from leaving the country. We stayed in this holding pattern, and it proved to be very difficult and humbling.

However, it also proved to be exactly what we needed as preparation for departing to the foreign mission field. During that time, in our holding pattern, I wrote and recorded my first solo album, *Just Let Go*. God grew us, stretched us, shaped up, built our faith and trust, and ultimately taught us to let go.

Still, it was hard. Month after month went by, and still I had no work permit. As April approached, we still hadn't sold our house, and there'd been little to no activity. I felt a bit like Job, when his friends were questioning his faith and the faithfulness of God. Some people thought the lack of work permit and the house not selling were signs that we were making the wrong decision.

But we'd burned our ships. We weren't looking back. We continued to believe that God had placed this call on our lives, even though our daily experience would have caused many people to doubt. I just had to learn to let go and trust God, and I believe God held out until I fully surrendered.

Eventually, I reached a breaking point where I laid myself before God in total surrender and released all of the expectations I had placed upon him. You see, because we were making such a big sacrifice, I felt entitled to ease. We were leaving everything to follow Jesus, so I thought we deserved a certain level of special treatment from God. I had to let go of all of those expectations. It was painful, but we finally did it.

A few days later, on Good Friday, we received three offers on our house, two of which were above the asking price. By Easter Sunday, we had a purchase agreement. Wow, what a profound metaphor!

It was a huge relief, a great gift, and a tremendous encouragement. Even so, it still took two more months for my work permit to come through, and we had to let go of those expectations as well. As it turns out, there were some things happening in Papua New Guinea with the role I was taking that made a July arrival much more appropriate. In fact, if we'd showed up earlier, our experience would have been very different, and possibly far less fruitful.

On July 18, 2010, we landed in Papua New Guinea for the first time, a country we had never been to before. Now, Papua New Guinea is a sub-third-world country, not advanced enough to be considered third world, and one of the top-five most corrupt countries in the world. Eighty percent of the people are stuck in ancient civilizations and practices and are only one short generation away from the practice of cannibalism.

Witchcraft, sorcery, and darkness reigned where there was no gospel. Tribal warfare, yes, with bows, arrows, spears, and knives, was still active. There were some guns such as 302s, MI6s, and I saw several homemade rifles (which were the scariest of them all because you never knew if they would blow up in your face). We personally witnessed the terrors of tribal fighting as it occurred multiple times where we lived.

Outside of that spiritual darkness, Papua New Guinea is one of the most beautiful, breathtaking, exotic creations of God. It is rich in culture and natural wonders, truly one of the most interesting, unique, and bizarre places I've ever been. And we were living there! We'd left home and said goodbye to family, liquidated everything, with the intent of staying in Papua New Guinea as long as God would have us stay.

It would take hundreds of pages to write about all of the stories and impactful things that happened to us during our three-year term in Papua New Guinea. God reshaped our hearts and gave us a new perspective that we could not have gained from any other experience.

He hit the reset button on our lives and taught us more about himself and how amazing the Christian walk is when you truly submit and follow him.

We learned how to live simply in 100 percent reliance on God's provisions. And while we had the least in terms of possessions, finances, and family that we'd ever had in our lives, we were content with what we had and felt blessed in abundance.

Living the Hard Sayings

It took many years of spiritual preparation and heart circumcision to get us to a place where we would faithfully respond when God called us to leave the comforts of home, give up everything, and follow him to Papua New Guinea. We had friends and family who disagreed with what we were doing. My career path and opportunities were already clear. Who would give that up?

During those six difficult months of waiting for my work permit, we had people ask us, "Are you sure you heard God correctly?" Some people from our church assumed we'd already left on our "mission trip" and returned, even though we were still waiting to leave. Our kids were two, five, and seven at the time, and a few people asked us why we would take little kids to such a dangerous place. "It's not fair to your children," they said.

All we could do was continually turn to the Word of God for encouragement. However, turning to the Word during that time really brought some of Jesus' more pointed teachings to light. Consider the following verses.

"And everyone who has left houses or brothers or sisters or father or mother or wife or children or fields for my sake will receive a hundred times as much and will inherit eternal life" (Matthew 19:29 ESV)[1].

*"No one can serve two masters, for either he will hate the one and love the other, or he will be devoted to the one and despise the other. You cannot serve God and money" (Matthew 6:24 ESV)[2].

*"Blessed are you when people insult you, persecute you and falsely say all kinds of evil against you because of me" (Matthew 5:11 NIV)[3].

"If anyone would come after me, let him deny himself and take up his cross

daily and follow me. For whoever would save his life will lose it, but whoever loses his life for my sake will save it" (Luke 9:23-24 ESV)[4].

"In the same way, those of you who do not give up everything he has cannot be my disciple" (Luke 14:33 NIV)[5].

"Anyone who loves his father or mother more than me is not worthy of me; anyone who loves his son or daughter more than me is not worthy of me; and anyone who does not take his cross and follow me is not worthy of me" (Matthew 10:37-39 NIV)[6].

"If you want to be perfect go sell your possessions and give to the poor, and you will have treasure in heaven. Then, come follow me" (Matthew 19:21 NIV)[7].

"The harvest is plentiful, but the workers are few. Ask the Lord of the harvest, therefore, to send out workers into his harvest field. Go! I am sending you like lambs among wolves" (Luke 10:1-3 NIV)[8].

"For it has been granted to you on behalf of Christ not only to believe in him, but to also suffer for him" (Philippians 1:29 NIV)[9].

"Consider it pure joy whenever you face trials of many kinds because you know that the testing of your faith produces perseverance" (James 1:2-3 NIV)[10].

"But even if you suffer for what is right you will be blessed" (1 Peter 3:14 NIV)[11].

"If you are insulted because of the name of Christ, you are blessed, for the Spirit of glory and of God rests on you...if you suffer as a Christian, do not be ashamed, but praise God that you bear that name" (1 Peter 4:14, 16 NIV)[12].

There are countless passages in the New Testament that talk about persecution and suffering for following Jesus. The book of Acts recounts stories of Christians suffering and being killed for their faith. This kind of persecution still happens in some parts of the world. It's not merely a thing of the past. Right now, as you read this, faithful believers are living under threat in some places because they follow Christ. And many of them have no material comforts to retreat to, but maybe that's a blessing in disguise.

I would hardly say we faced persecution, but it was not comparable to what the martyrs and many missionaries have dealt with. People have been tortured, starved, and put to death for their faith. This is the real potential cost of following Jesus. Sheep among wolves, as he put it.

As a business leader, what are you willing to give up to follow Jesus? Would you make a decision you knew was God's will even if it cost you dearly? What if it jeopardized your business? What if it brought lawsuits or bad press? What if you might lose your largest customer, or a key leader?

We probably won't get tortured and starved because of our faith in most places in America, but the type of persecution we face can still be devastating. Scripture tells us to expect it, so don't be surprised when things get hard because you choose to follow Jesus. We are to expect trials, suffering, or persecution—perhaps all three. I am convicted, and, to be honest, scared that if I'm not experiencing these things, I may not really be living out my faith.

Friends, whether you are a missionary on the foreign field or a business leader, all of the same Biblical principles apply. Why do we expect missionaries to give up everything, to embrace risk and potential persecution and suffering while we as leaders in America detach from these truths and retreat to comfort?

What if we as business leaders lived like missionaries in our context? If we have been blessed with an amazing job and income, how are we stewarding those resources? Are we stewarding them missionally, perhaps the same way a missionary would? When you're a missionary, you live off the money of others, so you have a constant feeling of needing to be faithful and frugal. Should we not view our "earned" money the same way? It's God's money, after all, given to us to steward for his purposes. Should we not still feel obligated to be faithful and frugal with that money? To put it to good work? To apply it faithfully to our ministry of reconciliation, whatever that is?

This is hard, especially when there is abundance. I found it much easier to have this mindset as a missionary when we didn't have much than I have as a business executive with so much. The parable of the poor widow in Luke 21 always strikes me. A widow had only two very small copper coins to give to the temple treasury, but she gave all she had. The rich people around her were giving huge sums of money, but what they gave was only a tiny percentage of their vast wealth.

And Jesus said, "Truly I tell you, this poor widow has put in more than all the others." In God's eyes, she gave more, and her gift made more of an impact for the Kingdom because it cost her more.

King David expresses a similar sentiment in 1 Chronicles 21, when a man named Araunah offers to give him oxen so he could make a burnt offering to the Lord. But King David replied to Araunah, "No, I insist on paying the full price. I will not take for the Lord what is yours, or sacrifice a burnt offering that costs me nothing" (1 Chronicles 21:24 NIV)[13]. David wound up paying 600 shekels of gold to the man, roughly fifteen pounds of gold, for something he could have gotten for free due to his kingly privilege. But he was giving to the Lord's purposes out of his abundance.

If we claim to follow Jesus, then these hard scriptures apply to the overseas missionary and the business leader, teacher, pastor, police officer, and every other believer in equal measure. That is the missional mindset.

I've gone from working in a business, to selling everything and moving to the foreign mission field. Then, I was led back to business to live out missions. Now, I was recently called back out of the family business to bring it all together and help others live and lead missionally. There are things that have been uncomfortable about all of those transitions. There have been great blessings and great challenges along the journey. These are just the large career moves, let alone the thousands of small decisions along the way that are simply navigating life, marriage, parenting and living on mission. Through all of which we have done our best to use the Bible as our compass, even the hard teachings we would rather ignore.

We can't simply apply the convenient, comforting, self-help verses of the Bible and ignore those clear teachings which are difficult to digest. When we have a missional mindset, we see ourselves as ambassadors of Christ who have been entrusted with the ministry of reconciliation in whatever context the Lord has placed us. We have a role in the Great Commission no matter our geographical location, job, or financial circumstances.

We are to focus on God, and he will provide the right context for us. He may call us to move far away, or he may ask us to stay right where we are. Either way, we need to wrestle with the truths in scripture and figure out how to live our lives in light of God's redemptive plan.

It's difficult, I know that, but I assure you, it's worth it. Please hear me on this. My most challenging and difficult days of following Jesus, serving him in hard places and uncertain times, brought a measure of blessing and fulfillment that cannot be found any other way. Jesus calls all of us to a life of surrender and obedience, and he has so much to give. He says in John 10:10 that he has come to bring life and bring it to the fullest!

No eye has seen, no ear has heard, what God has prepared for those who love him (1 Corinthians 2:9 NIV)[14]. So lean into the hard stuff, pray and ask God to help you process and apply every word of it. The Holy Spirit is alive and at work in each believer, but he will not force himself on us. Rather, we must yield and continually invite him into the inner spaces where he can lead us, guide us, and direct us in all things.

Questions to Prayerfully Consider

- Do you feel you take God's Word and apply all of it or just the parts that make sense or are comfortable?

- How do some of the more challenging verses about cost, sacrifice, and persecution make you feel? Take those honest feelings and questions to God in the form of a prayer in your journal.

- Do you believe following Jesus is worth it? If you are struggling, take that to God and ask for confidence and strength in the Lord. It's okay to feel weak and insufficient. It's in this humble state that God does his best work in us as he continues to prepare us for the good works he has planned for us.

- Regarding your business or position of leadership, would you do the right thing even if it had a significant cost? Would you follow the leading of the Holy Spirit to do something that might be controversial or costly?

- Are you willing to go? Are you willing to send others? Are you ready to view your life through the lens of the Great Commission and embrace God's heart for the world?

- Would you be willing to pray, send, give, or go to see the gospel expanded into the world? Are you ready to use what God has given you to be a part of accomplishing His mission?

12

A REVOLUTIONARY CALL

I would like to conclude by reflecting on the journey we have been through in this book and leave you with some pointed challenges. My hope is that inspiration will lead to action. That action may look different for every person, but my goal is to compel you in some way to keep unpacking the mystery and blessing of following Jesus.

I'm not talking about following Jesus the American pop-culture Christian way. I am talking about a following that consists of pursuing him and his Word with reckless abandon and complete surrender. There is both mystery and risk in following Jesus this way, and there is a cost we must consider. Will we choose to draw a line in the sand? Or will we give him the entire beach of our lives?

What do we mean by revolutionary call? God is calling us to something different than what the world has to offer. It's a challenge to go against the status quo, to turn things around, to go All In with our faith, and to live the life that Jesus is beckoning us to. It may seem radical or even foolish to the world, but normal and expected in the Kingdom of God. Being a missional leader shapes and influences how people think, and models how we are to live as we tap into the revolutionary power of Jesus.

Up to this point, I've shared many stories with the hope of inspiring and challenging your paradigm and perspective about what it means to be a Christian (and to further define that, a Christ-follower). What Jesus asks of us is clear, yet it's also a mystery. But we only need faith the size of a mustard seed to believe that God can do amazing, beautiful, and impactful work through us if we are yielded to the Holy Spirit. Imagine what your life, your work, and your business would look like if you were completely yielded to the Holy Spirit in all things, even the menial tasks.

It's impossible to manifest the great things God has placed in our hearts apart from Christ. We need him and the work of the Holy Spirit within us to produce the fruitfulness we desire. In John 15:5, Jesus says, "I am the vine, you are the branches. If a man remains in me and I in him, he will bear much fruit; apart from me you can do nothing."[1]

One of my favorite quotes of all time was by an evangelist named Henry Varley. This quote comes to us via D.L. Moody, who heard Henry speak while he was in England in the mid-1800s. It brings me to tears even as I write it:

"The world has yet to see what God can do through a [person] who is completely yielded to Him."

D.L. Moody responded to this quote by saying, "By the grace of God, may I be that man!"

This is the cry of my heart. I hope it inspires you to consider what's possible if you would completely yield to the Holy Spirit. Jesus is the only man who accomplished this in totality, but it is something to aspire to, to hope we can get as close as possible and share in that pursuit with courageous men such as D.L. Moody.

Other great leaders of the past faced impossible challenges that only God could overcome, and were given impossible visions that could only be carried out through complete surrender to the Holy Spirit. Following Jesus can be tough, and will probably get tougher, with greater sacrifices to come, but it's all for the sake of a legacy that will outlive us, usher in the Kingdom of Heaven, and prepare the way for Christ's return.

There is so much at stake! If God has positioned you as a leader over other people, then there is even more at stake. You have a great responsibility to steward what he has entrusted to you for the sake of the gospel. Don't take this lightly. The realization of how great the responsibility is should bring you to your knees. And that's what he wants! He wants us on our knees seeking him for discernment and direction about how we are to lead for his sake and his purposes.

Are you willing to risk it all to follow him and to make his name known among the nations? Are you willing to embrace discomfort, and perhaps persecution and suffering, for his name? Are you willing to give up what you feel you deserve to follow where he might be leading?

What if you chose to be all in and burn your ships? What ships would you need to burn and what's in them? And, are you currently building a ship that is pointed in the wrong direction?

What Are You Going to Do?

Of course, you can simply put this book down, say, "Well, that was kind of interesting," and then go back to living your life and leading your business as you were before. You can do nothing. However, I'm challenging you to deeply consider what you're willing to risk for the name of Jesus where he has placed you in life. Are there areas of your life or your work you haven't completely surrendered to him?

If you say that you believe in Jesus, then you have been commissioned as his ambassador and given the ministry of reconciliation. What are you doing about that? What am I doing about that? What are we doing together about that?

If we are to take the gospel to the ends of the Earth, if Christ's return hinges on all nations hearing of the gospel and then the end will come, what are you doing about that? How much time are you spending with God, seeking him, loving him, and asking him for guidance?

Maybe you're still the center of your story, in which case, you're probably not spending much time with him. However, if you will make Jesus the center of the story, then how can you do anything else but pursue him with all of your being?

How would your marriage change if you lived missionally? How would your relationships change? How would your parenting change? What would tomorrow look like for you at work if you walked through the door with a missional lens? What is the next incremental step you can take to move closer to Jesus? What are the things you are holding onto that you need to surrender?

My deepest desire is to walk in his presence as much as possible, even if that means he takes me to hard places, puts me in uncomfortable situations, or asks me to give up something I desire. This perspective has been shaped over the years of my journey because we've had success and wealth and we've also given up everything to follow him. It doesn't matter whether you live in America or somewhere else. It doesn't matter what you do for a living. The same radical commitment to Jesus and abandonment of the things of this world remain true for anyone who claims to be a Christian.

In February of 2023, I followed the call to step out from the security of a senior leadership role at our family business- a steady job, and steady income in order to launch Missional Leader. For the past several years I have wrestled with the longing to step away to launch a coaching organization to help others live out and integrate their faith in the marketplace, but at the same time knew God was holding me there until it was time to be released. There was still work to be done in me and through me at Wildman, and looking back, I can see that God was setting the table for what I am able to do today.

We want comfort, we want peace, we want harmony. But Jesus makes it clear that following him is costly. There will be suffering, there will be persecution, there will be discomfort, there will be division, potentially even among your family. If you really dig into the Scriptures and reflect on them, you must ponder the paradox of dying to live, of suffering to have joy, of living missionally to have fulfillment, and of laying down your life for our brothers and sisters for the sake of the gospel to find true purpose.

What's the bottom line? If we are seeking Jesus, then we are seeking to be connected to the vine so we can produce the fruit of good works that he has prepared in advance for us to do (Ephesians 2:10).

Life is challenging. Just surviving is a big enough challenge for some people. Are you confident that Jesus restores brokenness? That he redeems the lost and hurting? That he is a beacon of hope for everyone? If so, then you must share that hope, that message, that light with everyone.

How are you spending your time and resources, and to what end? Whose Kingdom are you building? An eternal Kingdom or a temporary Kingdom that is destined to perish?

Personally, the writing of this book has awakened my own sleeping senses. It caused me to reevaluate the ships I'm building that need to be burned. It has convicted me to stay on mission and not drift away into complacency and comfort.

I invite you—no, I challenge you—to continue this journey of exploration with me. I have more questions than answers, but I am on a quest to learn, discover, and apply the truth of scripture as best I can. Join me on the journey. Let's go all in. Let's live the Christian life to the fullest. Jesus said this is why he came.

All we have to do is abandon what the world offers us and choose to follow Jesus completely, whatever the cost. Together, let's create an All In Movement.

NOTES

Introduction

1. Matt. 7:21-23 NIV
2. 1 John 2:3-6 NIV
3. Matthew 28:19-20 (NIV)

1. The Center of Your Story

1. Psalm 19:1-4 NIV
2. Ephesians 2:8-10 (NIV)
3. 2 Cor. 4:6b-7 NIV
4. 2 Cor. 5:17-6:1 NIV
5. 1 Cor. 3:7-9 NIV
6. John 15:5 NIV

2. Burning Your Ships

1. Luke 9:57-62 ESV
2. Rev. 3:14-22 NIV
3. Isa. 29:13 NIV
4. 2 Chr. 16:9 NIV

3. The First Priority

1. 2 Cor. 4:16-18 NLT
2. Luke 14:15-24 ESV
3. Matt. 5:3 NIV
4. 1 Corinthians 9:24, 2 Timothy 4:8, Philippians 3:13-14, Galatians 5:7, and Hebrews 12:1-3
5. Rom. 12:2 NIV
6. Heb. 4:12 ESV
7. 2 Tim. 3:16 NIV
8. Rom. 12:2 ESV
9. Heb. 12:1-2 NIV
10. 1 Kin. 19:11-12 NIV
11. Phi. 4:6-7 NIV
12. Psa. 46:10 NIV
13. Psa. 27:14 NIV

4. Missional Family

1. Geoffrey Bromiley, *God and Marriage* (Michigan: William B. Eerdmans Publishing Company, 1980).
2. Eph. 5:21 NIV
3. Pro. 22:6 ESV
4. Deut. 6:5-9 NIV
5. Psa. 78:5-8 NLT

5. All In for Jesus

1. 2 Tim. 4:3 NIV
2. Dallas Willard, *The Spirit of the Discipline.* New York: HarperOne, 1999.
3. John 2:22 ESV
4. John 6:26 ESV
5. Statistics from *The Hole in Our Gospel: What Does God Expect of Us?* by Richard Stearns
6. Ralph Winter, "Missions Movement: War-Time Lifestyle, Christianity Today, 2023, https://www.christianitytoday.com/history/issues/issue-14/missions-movement-war-time-lifestyle.html.
7. David Platt, "Risk It All for Christian Mission." July 7, 2020, Toronto, Canada, 5:33, YouTube.

6. What If the Good News Was Really Good News?

1. Matt. 12:34-40 NIV
2. Rom. 1:16 ESV

7. God in Your Day Job

1. Timothy Keller, *Every Good Endeavor: Connecting Your Work to God's Work.* London: Penguin, 2014.
2. https://www.forbes.com/sites/susanadams/2014/06/09/how-unemployment-and-depression-fit-together
3. Romans 9:21 (NIV)
4. Col. 1:16-17 ESV
5. https://answersingenesis.org/environmental-science/stewardship/why-we-work/
6. Col. 3:17 NIV
7. Pro. 13:4 ESV
8. Eph. 4:28 ESV
9. 1 The. 4:11-12 ESV
10. 2 The. 3:10 ESV
11. Brother Lawrence, *The Practice of the Presence of God.* Pennsylvania: Whitaker House, 1982.

8. God Is the Owner

1. Matt. 19:26 NIV
2. Philippians 4:12 (NIV)

9. What If Love Works?

1. Graeme Goldsworthy, *According to Plan*. Illinois: IVP Academic, 2002.
2. "Workplace Stress," *The American Institute of Stress, https://www.stress.org/workplace-stress.*
3. Caitlin Mazur, "40+ Worrisome Workplace Stress Statistics," *Zippia,* last modified Feb. 11, 2023, https://www.zippia.com/advice/workplace-stress-statistics/.
4. https://www.businesswire.com/news/home/20200723005250/en/The-American-Worker-in-Crisis-Study-Finds-83-of-U.S.-Employees-Are-Experiencing-Mental-Health-Issues
5. Eph. 5:14-17 NIV
6. Pro. 3:27 NIV
7. Rom. 13:4-5 NIV
8. 1 John 3:18 NIV

10. The Most Important Results

1. Matt. 28:19 NIV
2. Matt. 24:14 NIV
3. Rev. 7:9 ESV
4. Matt. 6:33 ESV

11. The Hard Stuff

1. Matt. 19:29 ESV
2. Matt. 6:24 ESV
3. Matt. 5:11 NIV
4. Luke 9:23-24 ESV
5. Luke 14:33 NIV
6. Matt. 10:37-39 NIV
7. Matt. 19:21 NIV
8. Luke 10:1-3 NIV
9. Phil. 1:29 NIV
10. Jam. 1:2-3 NIV
11. 1 Pet. 3:14 NIV
12. 1 Pet. 4:14, 16 NIV
13. 1 Chr. 21:24 NIV
14. 1 Cor. 2:9 NIV

12. A Revolutionary Call

1.   John 15:5 NIV

ACKNOWLEDGMENTS

It was a dream in the back of my mind that some day I would write a book. Like most dreams unless someone challenges you to take a step, it remains a dream that eventually fades. This book was a result of a challenge from my friend and mentor Bill High. Thank you for presenting the challenge and giving me the confidence that I had something meaningful to share with the world.

I would also like to express my sincere appreciation to my wife, my kids, my family and my friends who have encouraged and supported me in launching Missional Leader and for giving me the courage to write a book. I would also like to thank my sweet and dear mother Rose. She has been a positive encouragement, supporter, and raving fan of most things in my life. She has also modeled what it looks like to sprinkle positivity and sunshine everywhere she goes.

I shared many stories of friends, family, and a few stories of those I don't even know personally. Thank you for giving me something to write about! Your courage, faithfulness, and desire to be "All In" are an inspiration to me, and I know will impact many others who read those stories in this book.

Thank you to Wildman Business Group and the many relationships that were forged over the years, and for the encouragement and support as I transitioned out of the business to start Missional Leader. I would like to especially thank my brother-in-law Josh Wildman for modeling and living out missional leadership as CEO of our family business. Many of the thoughts and concepts that were shared in this book we shaped together over years of brotherhood and working together.

Thank you to Steve and Pam Bryant who poured into me during my first decade in business. You believed in me from the start and have had my back through this entire journey.

Thank you to Brent Wildman for being a role model for me in life, for bringing me to Jesus as a 15 year old boy, and for being an inspiration for the entire Wildman family of what it looks like to have a fully surrendered heart.

ABOUT THE AUTHOR

Drew is the founder and CEO of Missional Leader, an organization focused on raising up missional leaders in the marketplace. He is on a relentless pursuit to bring a spiritual awakening and revival in the marketplace by raising up Missional Leaders who are committed to using their business and their sphere of influence to further the Great Commission.

Drew started his business career on the front lines, building a new business diversification of their family business from the ground up. As the business grew, he served in various executive and operational roles during his twenty years within the parent company, Wildman Business Group. At about the ten-year point, God called Drew out of the marketplace and into full-time ministry. He, his wife, and three kids at the time moved to the jungles of Papua New Guinea for three years to serve with Ethnos360 to help lead a mobilization program called Interface. Drew was then led back to the family business with a new call to live out missions through business.

After about ten years back at the company, Drew stepped away from his work within the family business to launch Missional Leader, putting the principles he learned in business and on the mission field to work. In addition to his business and missions experience, he is a certified Five Capitals Coach. He lives in Warsaw, IN with his wife Bobbi, and their four children.

About Missional Leader

Missional Leader offers executive coaching, roundtable groups, family legacy and succession coaching, experience trips, retreats, leadership workshops, and coaching around implementing faith-driven cultural programs.

Drew loves spending his time speaking, inspiring, and motivating people to go all in. Drew has a passion and gift for preaching, teaching, and speaking about many of the topics in this book, with a special emphasis on living and leading missionally. He speaks to various organizations, from corporate meetings and leadership conferences to churches and missionary training programs.

For more resources and information visit MissionalLeader.com.